Kurdistan Regional Government
Ministry of Planning

Making an Impact in the Kurdistan Region—Iraq

Summary of Four Studies to Assess the Present and Future Labor Market, Improve Technical Vocational Education and Training, Reform the Health Sector, and Build Data Collection Capacity

Sponsored by the Kurdistan Regional Government

C. Ross Anthony
Louay Constant
Shelby Culbertson
Peter Glick
Krishna B. Kumar
Robin C. Meili
Melinda Moore
Howard J. Shatz
Georges Vernez

RAND CORPORATION

For more information on this publication, visit www.rand.org/t/rr873

Library of Congress Cataloging-in-Publication Data
ISBN: 978-0-8330-8812-3

Published by the RAND Corporation, Santa Monica, Calif.
© Copyright 2015 Kurdistan Regional Government

RAND® is a registered trademark.

Limited Print and Electronic Distribution Rights

This document and trademark(s) contained herein are protected by law. This representation of RAND intellectual property is provided for noncommercial use only. Unauthorized posting of this publication online is prohibited. Permission is given to duplicate this document for personal use only, as long as it is unaltered and complete. Permission is required from RAND to reproduce, or reuse in another form, any of its research documents for commercial use. For information on reprint and linking permissions, please visit www.rand.org/pubs/permissions.html.

The RAND Corporation is a research organization that develops solutions to public policy challenges to help make communities throughout the world safer and more secure, healthier and more prosperous. RAND is nonprofit, nonpartisan, and committed to the public interest.

RAND's publications do not necessarily reflect the opinions of its research clients and sponsors.

Support RAND

Make a tax-deductible charitable contribution at
www.rand.org/giving/contribute

www.rand.org

Preface

Dr. Ali Sindi, Minister of Planning, on behalf of the Kurdistan Regional Government (KRG), asked the RAND Corporation to undertake several studies aimed at improving the economic and social development of the Kurdistan Region—Iraq (KRI). RAND's work is intended to help the KRG expand access to high-quality education and health care, increase private-sector development and employment for the expanding labor force, and design a data collection system to support high-priority policies.

This document provides an executive summary of four studies from Phase II of the research. The four individual studies are documented in the following reports:

- Howard J. Shatz, Louay Constant, Jill Luoto, Alexandria C. Smith, and Shmuel Abramzon, *An Assessment of the Present and Future Labor Market in the Kurdistan Region—Iraq: Implications for Policies to Increase Private-Sector Employment*, Santa Monica, Calif.: RAND Corporation, RR-489-KRG, 2014.
- Louay M. Constant, Shelly Culbertson, Cathleen Stasz, and Georges Vernez, *Improving Technical Vocational Education and Training in the Kurdistan Region—Iraq*, Santa Monica, Calif.: RAND Corporation, RR-277-KRG, 2014.
- C. Ross Anthony, Melinda Moore, Lee H. Hilborne, and Andrew W. Mulcahy, *Health Sector Reform in the Kurdistan Region—Iraq: Financing Reform, Primary Care, and Patient Safety*, Santa Monica, Calif., RAND Corporation, RR-490-KRG, 2014.
- Shmuel Abramzon, Nicholas E. Burger, Bonnie Ghosh-Dastidar, Peter Glick, Krishna B. Kumar, Francisco Perez-Arce, and Alexandria C. Smith, *Capacity Building at the Kurdistan Regional Statistics Organization Through Data Collection*, Santa Monica, Calif.: RAND Corporation, RR-293-KRG, 2014.

We expect this summary document to be of interest to policymakers in the KRG, as well as to a broad audience concerned with social and economic reform in the KRI.

The research documented in these reports and summarized in this volume was sponsored by the KRG and conducted by the RAND Corporation. For more information about the studies or about the RAND Corporation, please contact Robin Meili, director of International Programs, by email at Robin_Meili@rand.org, by phone at +1-310-393-0411 extension 7190, or by mail at the RAND Corporation, 1776 Main Street, P.O. Box 2138, Santa Monica, CA 90407-2138. More information about RAND is available at www.rand.org.

Contents

Figures and Tables

Figures

Tables

Acknowledgments

The entire RAND study team is grateful to the Kurdistan Regional Government (KRG) for supporting this research. Our team is particularly indebted to the generous sponsorship, and assistance of His Excellency Dr. Ali Sindi, Minister of Planning, who supported our work, provided guidance and feedback throughout these studies, and facilitated our interactions with officials in government and the private sector. We also thank His Excellency Dr. Rekawt H. Rashid, Minister of Health, as well as His Excellency Taher Hawrami, former Minister of Health. We thank His Excellency Mr. Safeen M. Dizayee, Minister of Education, during the first part of our study, and His Excellency Dr. Asmat Muhamad Khalid, Minister of Education, during the second part of our study. Within the Ministry of Planning (MOP), we are deeply grateful to Mr. Zagros Fatah Siwaily, Director General of the Capital Investment Budget and former Director General of Development Coordination and Cooperation, and Mr. Serwan Mohammed, Director of the Kurdistan Regional Statistics Office (KRSO) for always being available to provide insightful comments, feedback, and wise guidance throughout this research. We are appreciative of the diligent review of Dr. Jamal Ameen, Senior Advisor. We are also grateful for the unceasing efforts and translations services of the MOP staff, including Mr. Worya Ahmed, Mr. Hoshyar Aziz, Mr. Omar Abit, Mr. Muhammad A. Ahmed, and Mr. Farhad Borhan Qadir, who facilitated our work in the Kurdistan Region—Iraq (KRI).

The four study teams would also like to acknowledge the following individuals and organizations for their support.

Assessing the Present and Future Labor Market. We wish to acknowledge the enormous effort by Mr. Serwan Mohamed, Director of the KRSO, and his staff, especially Mr. Muhsin, Mr. Gohdar, and Mr. Hawraz, for assisting us in obtaining the data we required. We are also grateful to Dr. Haitham Numan of ASHARQ Co. Ltd. and his staff for expertly fielding a firm-level survey for us and working closely with us to ensure its success.

We thank staff of the Ministry of Education (MOE), Ministry of Higher Education and Scientific Research (MOHESR), Ministry of Labor and Social Affairs, and Ministry of Trade and Industry for providing the information we required for this research. In particular, we thank Mr. Maqsood S. Mohammed and Dr. Fatima R. Hasan Bajalani for their responsiveness and support throughout.

Improving Technical and Vocational Education and Training. We wish to thank His Excellency Dr. Asmat Muhamad Khalid, Minister of Education during this study. Within the MOE, we also thank Mr. Yosuif Othman Yosuif, Director General of Planning; Mr. Ahmed Ismail Rahman, Director General of Secondary and Vocational School; Mr. Yousif Abdullah Mohammed, Director of Vocational Education; Mr. Kafi Attallah Ahmed, Director of Statistics; and Ms. Dastan A. Ali, Senior Coordinator. We also extend our gratitude to Mr. Haji Rasul Ali, Director General, Ministry of Labor and Social Affairs; Dr. Kawther Aziz Galaly,

President of the Foundation of Technical Education, Erbil; and Dr. Nasih Othman, Vice President of the Foundation of Technical Education, Sulaimaniya, MOHESR. The many dedicated KRI technical vocational education and training administrators, principals, professors, and teachers who shared their experience and concerns with us also deserve special recognition.

At RAND, we are grateful to Drs. Jill Luoto and Howard Shatz for their work on the development of the survey of employers and analysis of the data and to Beth Katz, who participated in the country case studies of technical and vocational education and training systems. We are also indebted to Dr. Haitham Numan of ASHARQ Co. Ltd. and his staff for the fielding of the employer survey.

Health Sector Reform. We would like to express our great appreciation for the invaluable assistance of all the health professionals living in the KRI who were extremely helpful to us during the study. We are indebted to all of the Ministry of Health (MOH) staff who assisted us; in particular, we would like to thank His Excellency Dr. Rekawt H. Rashid, Minister of Health, as well as His Excellency Dr. Taher Hawrami, former Minister of Health, both of whom provided us with invaluable feedback and direction. We would also like to express our great appreciation for the invaluable assistance of all the health professionals living in the KRI who were extremely helpful to us during the study.

Many other people were extremely helpful during this study. We thank the entire staff of the MOH and, in particular, the various Directors General for all of their assistance in the overall study and in helping to secure the management information data requested. Very special thanks are also due to Dr. Amer Omar for acting as our primary contact within the MOH and for his tireless assistance.

Capacity Building at the KRSO Through Data Collection. We are indebted to Mr. Serwan Mohamed, Director of the KRSO. We could not have met as many KRG officials as we did during our visits to the KRI without the unceasing efforts of the MOP staff mentioned above.

We also want to acknowledge the talented and dedicated staff of the KRSO, whose hard work made the first Kurdistan Regional Labor Force Survey a success. In particular, we would like to thank Mr. Gohdar Mohammad Ali Saeid, Mr. Raqeeb Bahaadin Mohammed, Mr. Saman Ahmad, Ms. Fatma Omer Ali, Mr. Bashdar Ayub Kareem, Mr. Soran Habib, Mr. Shwan Abbas Khudhur, and Ms. Nahema Akram Jabar.

Abbreviations

A-NHS	Accountable National Health Service
DOH	Department of Health
GRP	gross regional product
IHSES	Iraq Household Socio-Economic Survey
ISCED	International Standard Classification of Education
KRG	Kurdistan Regional Government
KRI	Kurdistan Region—Iraq
KRLFS	Kurdistan Region Labor Force Survey
KRSO	Kurdistan Region Statistics Office
LMIS	Labor-Market Information System
LMO	labor-market observatory
MIS	management information system
MOE	Ministry of Education
MOF	Ministry of Finance
MOH	Ministry of Health
MOHESR	Ministry of Higher Education and Scientific Research
MOLSA	Ministry of Labor and Social Affairs
MOP	Ministry of Planning
PHC	primary health care center
SHI	social health insurance
TVET	technical and vocational education and training
UNIDO	United Nations Industrial Development Organization

CHAPTER ONE

Introduction

This executive summary describes key results from four studies carried out by RAND as part of Phase II of its work for the Kurdistan Regional Government (KRG).

Assessing the Present and Future Labor Market in the KRI

The first study, described in Chapter Two, addresses the question of how the KRG can improve the private-sector labor market in the Kurdistan Region—Iraq (KRI). Policymakers want to guide the KRI toward a private-sector–driven economy. Doing so will involve creating a mechanism by which job-seekers can develop the right skills and find employers who will hire them, employers can find the employees they need, and the government can create an enabling environment in which the best matches between job-seekers and employers can be made.

Improving Technical and Vocational Education and Training in the KRI

The KRI is enjoying rapid economic growth, but the lack of skilled workers may constrain continued growth. As part of its sweeping efforts to transform and grow the KRI's education system, the KRG asked RAND to assess its technical and vocational education and training (TVET) system. The study described in Chapter Three fulfills that request and recommends measures to increase TVET quality and access.

Health Sector Reform in the KRI

The KRG asked RAND to support its efforts to reform the health system in the KRI. The study described in Chapter Four provides an analysis of three key distinct but intertwined health policy areas (financing, primary care, and patient safety and quality) that need to be addressed as the KRG continues to improve the KRI health care system.

Capacity Building at the Kurdistan Region Statistics Office Through Data Collection

In a previous study, RAND assessed institutional arrangements and the data and infrastructure available for collecting and sharing data within the KRI; identified KRG policy priorities and data items to be collected for each priority area; and recommended data collection methods, institutional arrangements, and steps needed to build capacity within the Kurdistan Region Statistics Office (KRSO). In the study described in Chapter Five, RAND assisted the KRSO and the KRG in building the capacity to undertake the recommended data collection, and worked closely with the KRSO and the relevant ministries to prepare, conduct, and analyze the first round of the Kurdistan Region Labor Force Survey (KRLFS).

Methods

The four studies summarized here have employed multiple research methods.

Assessing the Present and Future Labor Market. For this study, researchers analyzed a number of data sources, including data from the KRG Ministry of Education (MOE), Ministry of Higher Education and Scientific Research (MOHESR), and the KRLFS. RAND also used data from the Iraq Household Socio-Economic Survey (IHSES) 2007 and the RAND Survey of Business Establishments 2012. In cooperation with the KRG, RAND conducted a survey of 360 business establishments in the KRI. Researchers also conducted interviews with officials in government, the private sector, and universities. RAND also drew on data about other countries from various sources, including the World Bank; the International Monetary Fund; the Center for International Comparisons of Production, Income and Prices at the University of Pennsylvania; the Organisation for Economic Co-operation and Development; and the International Labour Organization, and reviewed documents from the KRI and the international policy and research literature.

Improving Technical Vocational Education and Training. To assess the current TVET system in the KRI and make recommendations for its improvement, RAND undertook several tasks. These included a literature review on effective TVET systems, analyses of secondary data on TVET programs in the KRI, interviews with leaders and staff of the KRI ministries responsible for TVET, case studies of TVET systems in other countries, and a survey of KRI employers on their workforce needs.

Health Sector Reform. RAND researchers analyzed three distinct but intertwined health policy issue areas: financing policy development, implementation of early primary care recommendations, and quality and patient safety assessment and recommendations. In all three areas, RAND researchers examined each issue, reviewed the relevant literature, explored the issue in discussions with key stakeholders, developed and assessed various policy options, and developed plans or approaches to overcome barriers and achieve stated policy objectives. In the area of primary care, they developed and helped to implement a new management information system.

Capacity Building at the KRSO. This study involved the following activities, with capacity building being deeply involved in all: (1) design of the KRLFS sampling approach; (2) development of the survey questionnaire; (3) data collection, cleaning, and validation; (4) analysis of KRLFS data to assess key labor force indicators; and (5) development of recommendations for a KRI establishment survey that would enable the calculation of a reliable measure of gross regional product for the KRI. Activities 1 through 4 were carried out in close collaboration with the KRSO during a series of five intensive workshops held at KRSO headquarters (with attendance ranging from 15 to 30 staff) and through frequent communications over the life of the study. The KRSO carried out the first KRLFS round successfully in July 2012 and the second in December 2012.

CHAPTER TWO

Assessing the Present and Future Labor Market in the KRI

The KRI is developing rapidly. Fueled by its natural resource wealth, the economy is growing, especially in infrastructure and services. Although a large share of the economy remains in the government sector, the KRG has been promoting a larger role for the private sector. To develop a private sector that can further fuel and sustain this economic growth, KRG policymakers will need to take steps to develop a more robust labor market that can supply the necessary skills. This study addresses the issue of how the KRG can promote a labor market that is responsive to the needs of the private sector.

To develop a more robust private-sector labor market, three goals should be pursued. First, job-seekers will need to acquire the necessary skills that meet employer demand and that can be deployed on the job readily. Second, employers should be able to make job-seekers aware of jobs and should be able to find the employees who possess the needed skills. Third, government policies should create an enabling environment in which the best matches between job-seekers and employers can be made.

RAND conducted four tasks to help inform policymaking in these areas. First, we estimated the likely number and education levels of new job-seekers through 2020. Second, we conducted an original scientific survey of employers to learn about labor demand. Third, we investigated sectoral employment growth in comparison economies to identify promising growth sectors in the KRI. Finally, we outlined policy steps for the government to consider, including establishing a Labor-Market Information System (LMIS) to support policymaking and improve the functioning of the private-sector labor market.

Well-functioning private-sector labor markets strongly benefit from broader government policies, such as those related to business regulation, financial markets, and the legal system. Although we did not examine these issues within the scope of this study, we recognize that the labor-market policies we discuss are linked to broader policy actions and therefore constitute a useful but not complete program for improving the private-sector labor market. Other steps are described more fully in other research that RAND has done for the KRG (Hansen et al., 2011).

We rely on a number of data sources in this study:

- MOE enrollment data for basic and secondary grades
- MOHESR enrollment data for all public higher-education institutions in the KRI
- KRLFS 2012 (KRSO, 2012)
- IHSES 2007
- The RAND Survey of Business Establishments 2012 (The RAND Skills Survey; RAND Corporation, 2012)
- interviews with officials in government, the private sector, and universities

- existing secondary datasets
- document review.

The Composition of the Labor Force Is Changing

According to recent data, the majority of the KRI labor force has up to a grade 6, or primary, education. Trends suggest that new labor-market entrants will be much better educated than the current labor market. The KRG has carried out a number of initiatives to universalize education, and in 2007 made education through grade 9 compulsory, up from grade 6. In addition, the population is expanding, as is the number of postsecondary education institutions. These changes are likely to have a long-term effect on the labor market by increasing the education of the workforce.

As shown in Figure 2.1, we estimate that the number of labor-market entrants with two-year and four-year post-secondary degrees should increase. We project that, from late 2012 through 2020, at least 215,700 people with a postsecondary degree, or about 24,000 people each year, will move directly from the education system to the labor force. We project that this will include 85,000 graduates of two-year institutions. We also project that this will include 130,100 university graduates.

We estimate that the number of new labor-market entrants with only a grade 9 education will be smaller than the number of labor-market entrants from the upper grade levels. We proj-

Figure 2.1
Estimated Number of People Entering the Labor Market After Completing Two-Year and Four-Year Postsecondary Degrees

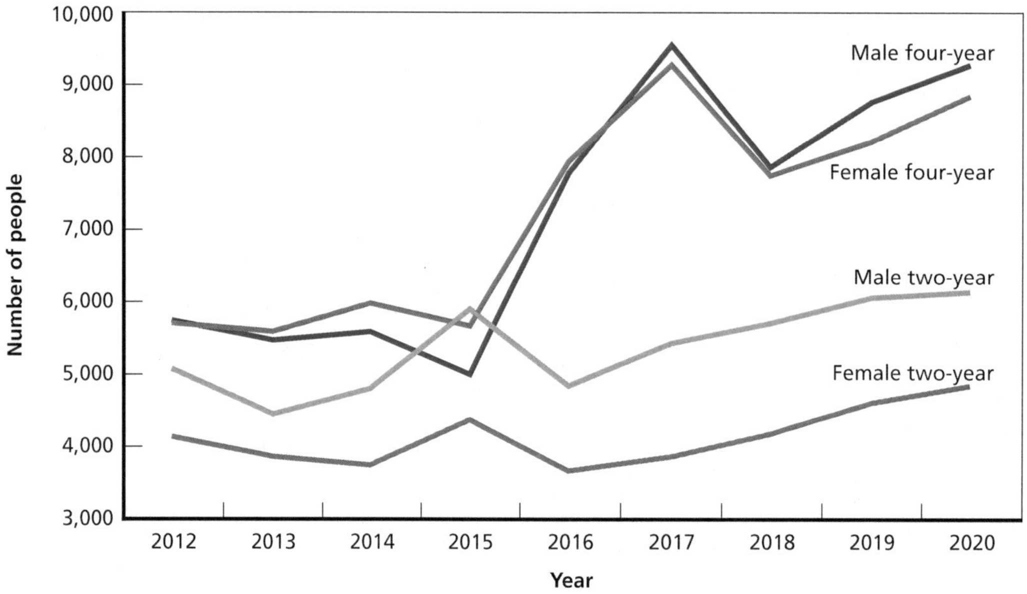

SOURCE: Authors' computations based on data from MOHESR and the KRSO, 2012.
NOTES: Data are insufficient to allow us to explain the large increase and then dip in labor force participation in 2017 and 2018 among people enrolled in four-year institutions, and the temporary increase in labor force participation in 2015 among people enrolled in two-year institutions.
RAND *RR873-2.1*

ect that, from late 2012 through 2020, approximately 44,600 to 51,500 people will enter the labor market immediately after leaving school with a grade 9 education. In contrast, we project that approximately 127,000 to 137,000 people (14,000 to 15,200 annually) will enter the labor market immediately after leaving school with a grade 12 education.

The ability of those with only a grade 9 education to find jobs will depend not only on the extent to which private businesses need low-skilled workers, but also the extent to which such businesses prefer foreign low-skilled workers. Currently, many foreign workers come from Turkey, but also from Lebanon, Uganda, Nepal, Sri Lanka, and many other countries.

Employers Demand Technical Knowledge, Practical Experience, and Soft Skills

Beyond examining changes to the composition of the KRI labor force, we conducted a baseline assessment of employer demand for skills using a survey of 360 employers. In our survey, we gathered data on the following areas: workforce composition (including education and nationality), hiring plans and practices, skills in greatest demand, challenges hiring within the KRI, types of occupations most difficult to fill, perceived labor force gaps, and employer-provided training. We also interviewed numerous employers about these issues.

The majority of employers in the survey rated graduates as prepared for work. However, 40 percent noted inadequate preparation of graduates at the secondary level. One-third indicated that they plan to hire non-KRI nationals to meet their future workforce needs. Large companies seem to be the main source of hiring outside the KRI and are also potentially an important source of future jobs.

About 25 percent of employers said that they faced difficulties in hiring from within the KRI for jobs that require a secondary school degree (general or vocational). Those who did cited as reasons lack of experience (40 percent), lack of educational qualifications (31 percent), and skill shortcomings (21 percent) (Figure 2.2). The most frequently cited occupations for which it was difficult to find local staff were the technical ones (for example, master technicians and engineering technicians). In interviews, employers emphasized the need for basic vocational and technical skills that are in high demand in the labor market.

Our analysis of the interviews and the survey further emphasized the importance that employers give to "soft" skills, such as communications and interpersonal interaction, as well as to work ethic, teamwork, and problem solving. As shown in Table 2.1, employers emphasized some skills for all employees, including customer handling[1]; communication skills, such as written and oral communications; and willingness to work hard. Employers had additional expectations for postsecondary graduates, including the ability to work with numbers ("numeracy") and English-language skills, coupled with some practical technical experience.

A modest share of employers (20 percent) provide training to their employees, and when it is provided, it is generally in areas specifically related to the job rather than in developing soft skills or language skills. Employers cited lack of funds, inability to spare staff time, and lack of training options in areas of need as constraints to providing training to employees.

[1] Customer handling refers to professionally dealing with customers, addressing their concerns, and solving their problems, and may involve interaction face-to-face, over the phone, or in writing.

Figure 2.2
For Employers Reporting Difficulties, Reasons for Difficulties Hiring for Jobs Requiring a Secondary School Degree with Candidates from the KRI

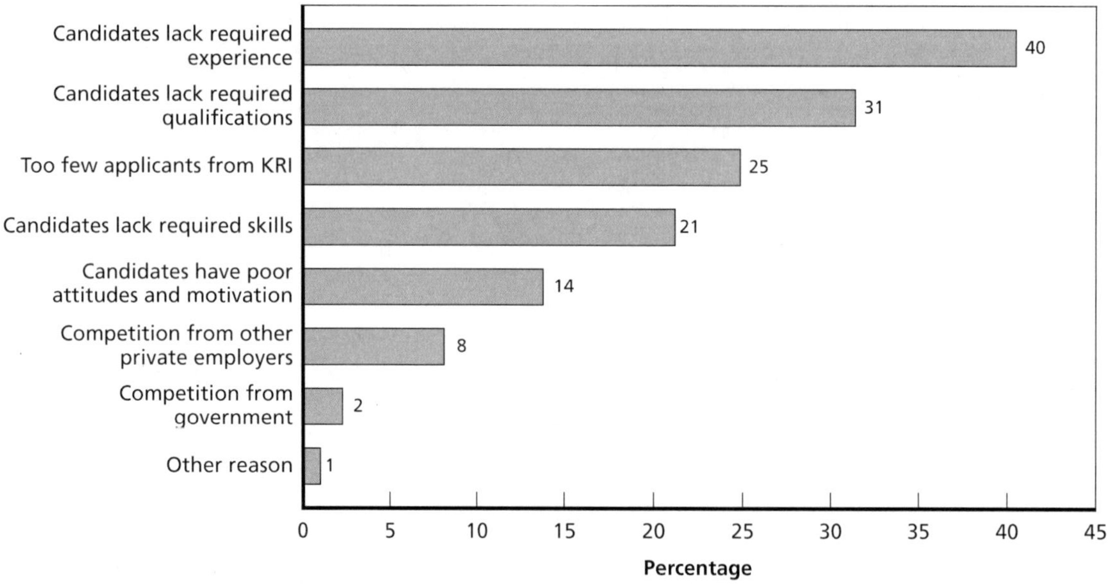

SOURCE: RAND Corporation, 2012.
NOTES: Question: What are the main difficulties behind being able to fill those vacancies with Iraqi Nationals from the Kurdistan Region? (n = 83). Percentages shown are conditioned on employers responding that they face difficulties hiring for jobs requiring a secondary school degree. A majority of employers did not respond that they faced difficulties and thus were not asked the question on the reasons for the hiring difficulties.
RAND *RR873-2.2*

Table 2.1
Most Important Skills, as Identified by Employers, by Level of Schooling Required for the Job

Skill	Percentage
Secondary Education	
Customer handling	42
Willingness to work hard	32
Written communications	32
Oral communications	29
Postsecondary Education	
Practical technical experience	24
English	21
Numeracy	21
Customer handling	21

SOURCE: RAND Corporation, 2012.

NOTE: The table shows the percentage of times 360 employers chose a particular skill as one of the top three most important skills for job applicants to possess.

Employment Is Likely to Grow Most Rapidly in Such Service Sectors as Construction, Transportation, and Domestic Trade

The employer survey provided insight into skills in demand now and potentially in the future. This can help KRG policymakers improve the educational system to supply the desired skills. Another approach is to consider which sectors are most likely to grow as a way to identify where the new graduates through 2020 are likely to find employment.

To understand potential futures for the economy of the KRI, we drew on historical evidence about how employment in small and medium-sized resource-rich economies developed. We selected a set of countries with characteristics similar to those of the KRI.[2] We investigated the evolution of employment in those economies in major sectors and in manufacturing industries, focusing on sectors and industries that were large and had experienced above-average employment growth.

Three major sectors experienced above-average employment growth across a large number of countries and time periods: (1) construction; (2) transport, storage, and communications; and (3) wholesale and retail trade. These sectors are already growing rapidly in the KRI. KRG policymakers have been emphasizing manufacturing and agriculture as high-priority sectors for employment growth. We found that in some countries, these sectors grew in terms of employment. But rarely did both grow rapidly in a single economy; more commonly, services sectors were the leading growth sectors for employment.

Seven manufacturing industries have shown a tendency toward above-average employment growth in the comparison economies (Figure 2.3): (1) food and beverage manufacturing; (2) non-metallic mineral products; (3) basic metals; (4) fabricated metal products; (5) chemicals and chemical products; (6) rubber and plastics products; and (7) transport equipment other than motor vehicles, trailers, and semi-trailers. Some of these industries may be well placed to grow in the KRI. These include food and beverage manufacturing, given the KRI's agricultural resources; non-metallic mineral products, given the KRI's mineral resources; and both the chemical products industry—which includes petrochemicals—and the rubber and plastics products industry, given the KRI's access to petroleum resources.

Labor Market Information Systems Can Monitor Labor Market Performance

The study shows that the KRI's labor market and economy are changing rapidly, and it is useful to collect and analyze data on supply and demand for skills to formulate effective labor-market policies. In their effort to develop better labor-market information, many countries have designated public offices to be responsible for collecting and compiling labor-market data, similar to the new responsibility of conducting quarterly labor force surveys, which is assigned to the KRSO. These offices or departments can compile and analyze labor-market data to help inform decisionmaking by employers, employees, educational institutions, policymakers, and others involved in the labor market.

---

[2] There were 14 comparison countries: Algeria, Argentina, Azerbaijan, Chile, Colombia, Ecuador, Guatemala, Kazakhstan, Malaysia, Peru, Romania, South Africa, Tunisia, and Venezuela. These economies have varied economic, geographic, and cultural characteristics. They share with the KRI such characteristics as significant natural resource extraction, employment in tourism, and the potential for sizable agricultural sectors.

Figure 2.3
Manufacturing Industries with Above-Average Employment Growth and a Substantial Share of Employment (Number of Occurrences in Nine Countries)

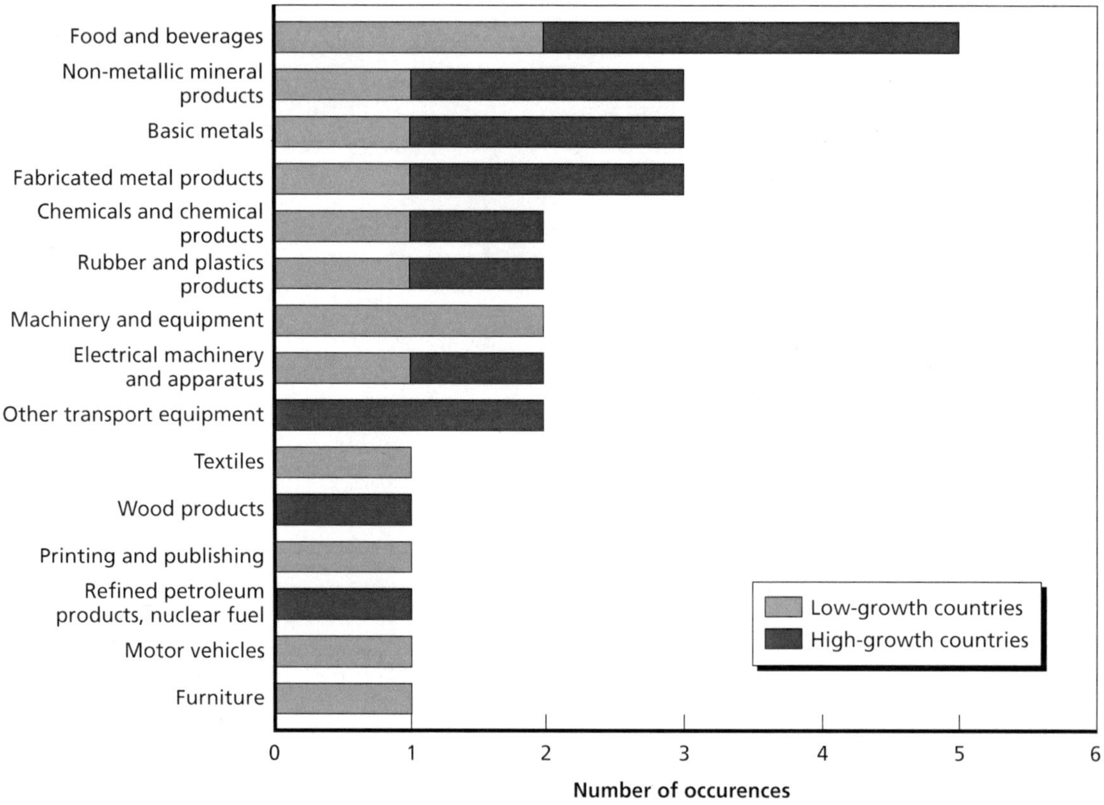

SOURCES: Authors' analysis based on United Nations Industrial Development Organization (UNIDO), 2012; United Nations Statistics Division, undated.
NOTES: (1) An occurrence is counted when an industry employs more than 5 percent of a country's manufacturing sector employees and when its employment grows faster than that of the whole manufacturing sector. (2) The countries in the sample and the time periods for which they have data are Argentina (1995–2002), Azerbaijan (1995–2009), Colombia (2000–2005), Ecuador (1995–2008), Kazakhstan (1998–2007), Malaysia (2000–2008), Romania (2003–2008), South Africa (1995–2009), and Tunisia (1995–2002). (3) The following eight industries did not have any occurrences and do not appear in the graph: tobacco products; wearing apparel, fur; leather, leather products, and footwear; paper and paper products; office, accounting, and computing machinery; radio, television, and communication equipment; medical, precision, and optical instruments; and recycling.
RAND *RR873-2.3*

The institutional arrangements and procedures that coordinate the collection, processing, storage, retrieval, and dissemination of labor-market information are known collectively as a Labor Market Information System. A well-functioning LMIS that provides labor-market information analysis and dissemination could help the KRG develop data-driven policies that support its goals of private-sector development and job creation. Figure 2.4 demonstrates the intended flow of information from the various sources within the KRI that would supply a hypothetical LMIS, the integration and processing of those data by the LMIS office, and the outcomes and users of the information processed by the LMIS.

An ideal LMIS is made up of seven elements grouped into three categories: (1) labor supply (labor statistics, education, and qualification statistics; register of foreign residents); (2) labor demand (labor-market needs assessments); and (3) labor-market matching (register of job-seekers and job offers, information provided by private placement agencies). The KRG

Figure 2.4
Labor Market Information System Process Flow Diagram

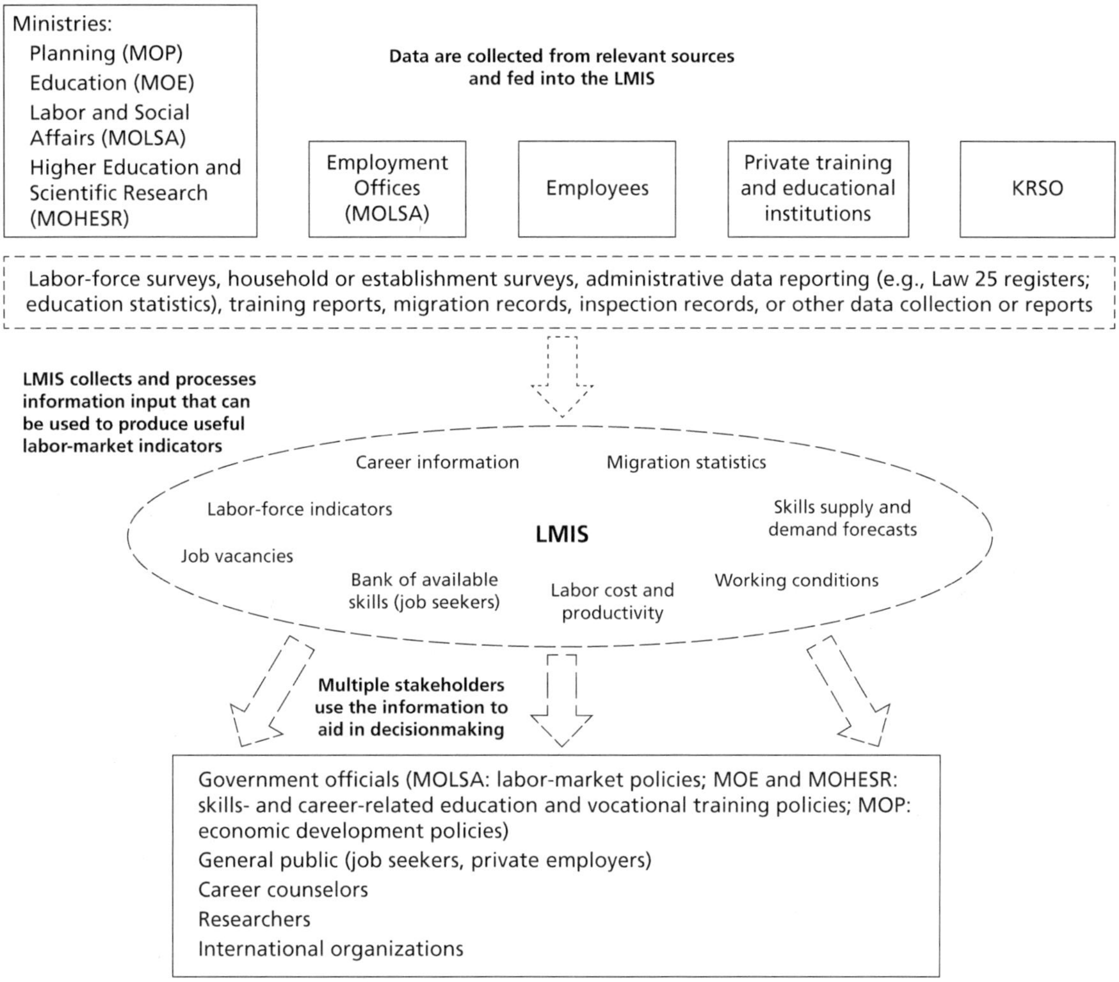

SOURCE: Authors' analysis of LMIS literature.
RAND *RR873-2.4*

has already made progress in assembling some of these elements through labor force surveys, availability of administrative education data, and the new labor exchange, Kurdistan Works.

In addition to these seven elements, an LMIS is generally run by a labor-market observatory (LMO), which collects information from various sources and then processes and analyzes it to put the data in a usable format for the intended users of an LMIS. The success of an LMO, as well as the overall success of an LMIS, depends in large part on the degree to which the LMO is able to effectively coordinate across different government ministries and between the public and private sectors.

Despite the current popularity of LMISs, there is no consensus among labor-market researchers as to their actual economic effects. Although there is no evidence that LMISs worsen labor-market outcomes, there is a lack of rigorous evaluations on their effects or cost-effectiveness. A number of studies provide evidence that the availability of labor-market information improves the functioning of labor markets and that elements of LMISs, such as job-search assistance, can improve labor-market outcomes (Woods and O'Leary, 2006, cited in

Murray, 2010). However, other research also finds that LMISs often fail and that the difficulty of establishing them is often underestimated (Johanson, 2002).

Suggested Policy Actions for the KRG to Meet Private-Sector Labor-Market Needs

KRG policymakers can take a number of steps to improve the labor market for the benefit of the private sector.

Policy Directions Relevant to the Postsecondary Education System

Although the system is producing graduates, there is room to improve their preparation for the workforce. Recent reforms to the higher education system have been implemented partly to address many of the problems highlighted by employers. But the higher education system can take further steps.

Build links with the private sector through private-sector advisory boards. These can establish ongoing input into curriculum and program decisions that will help students become better prepared for the demands of the private-sector labor market.

Build links with the private sector through career centers and job fairs. Career centers can help teach students how to look for work, where potential job opportunities are, and how to better prepare themselves for their lives after education. Job fairs can provide a mechanism for matching employers with job-seekers and educate students about opportunities.

Improve student work experience through expanded and improved internships. The survey and interviews showed that employers value some amount of work experience. This experience can be gained through internships. University career centers can take the lead in strengthening current internship opportunities by working with employers and students to raise expectations about what should result from an internship. The next step would be to learn from these experiences to expand successful approaches over time.

Policy Directions Relevant to All Segments of the Current and Future Labor Market

Institute a regular labor-market needs assessment survey. Many of our recommendations for improving the labor supply are derived from findings of the survey. Regular systematic data collection activities should be conducted to gather information about labor-market needs. The data collected can be used to understand emerging trends and help plan education and training.

Focus on the development of skills that are applicable to a broad selection of likely growth sectors. Our analysis of other economies suggests that the most likely large employment gains will come in such sectors as construction; transportation, storage, and communications; and wholesale and retail trade. To gain advantage from these likely growth sectors and yet still retain the possibility of having a workforce prepared for the favored sectors of manufacturing, agriculture, and tourism, KRG policymakers should make sure that education and training include skills applicable to a broad range of sectors.

Guard against barriers to the growth of manufacturing and agriculture. Barriers could include skills gaps, an unfavorable regulatory environment, or poor trade infrastructure. Skill development in the KRI should not be tailored to or focused only on these sectors. In addition, many of the skills for these sectors could be taught at high-quality secondary vocational schools and postsecondary technical institutes and colleges.

Continue reforms of government hiring. Government employment is still seen as the preferred employment option by many graduates of the postsecondary education system and even of the secondary education system. The KRG has expressed a desire to limit the expansion of the public sector and has received a plan to do so from earlier work by RAND. The KRG should continue to work within these plans to reform its government employment practices.

Steps to Consider for a KRG LMIS

If the KRG is considering whether to establish an LMIS, we recommend that it take the following steps. Even if the KRG determines that it will not create an LMIS, it would benefit from carrying out the steps below that relate to data collection and dissemination.

Fully consider the costs and benefits of developing an LMIS. An LMIS could prove to be of value by creating an agency that provides a central point of coordination and develops analytical capabilities that would take full advantage of the variety of data available. However, such an agency could also prove costly, fail to attract qualified individuals, fail to coordinate appropriately, and unnecessarily limit the availability of data to users. If establishing an LMIS is judged to be appropriate, then the KRG should proceed with the next steps.

Create an action plan for developing a KRI-wide LMIS, the first step of which should be to determine a structure for an LMO that will operate the LMIS. Decisions to be made for the LMO include in which ministry or ministries it will reside, how it will be funded and staffed, and how it will achieve institutional cooperation. After the LMIS and LMO begin operations, the plan should be to gradually add to the functions and capacities of the LMIS as the LMO gains experience and as it builds the necessary inter-institutional coordination framework.

Build a website (or expand the website of the KRSO) to make available all existing resources on labor-market information. This new website can serve as the basis for an LMIS and begin the process of information flow between suppliers of the information and the various users. In addition, it can serve as the first publicly available single-source resource for up-to-date and comprehensive information on the private-sector economy within the KRI.

Build a qualifications registry by establishing a data-sharing agreement with the KRI's education and training institutions. This may be done either directly or via existing data-sharing arrangements between the MOE, the MOHESR, and the schools.

Work with KRG's residency and border control agencies to collect data on the entry of foreign workers. Since the KRI is home to an increasing number of immigrants, both from other parts of Iraq as well as from outside countries, it is becoming increasingly important for the KRG to keep records of the numbers and skills of these immigrants to have a reliable portrait of the available stock of labor within the KRI.

Have the LMO institute regular labor-market needs assessments in different sectors. This will update and improve on the baseline findings conducted by RAND on labor-market needs and skills gaps. Since the KRI's economy is undergoing rapid expansion and changes, it is imperative that the understanding of skills gaps and private-sector labor-market needs be updated periodically to remain relevant and informative.

Have the LMO work with private employment placement agencies to create a mechanism for sharing information with the newly established LMIS. Since private employment agencies are active within the KRI's private-sector economy, having a window into their activities will be crucial as the private sector continues to develop rapidly within the KRI.

After an LMIS is fully functioning in its role of offering policy support, have the LMO explore creating links to or integrating the labor-market matching function for today's employment needs. Data-sharing links could be developed so that the LMIS gains greater visibility into job applicants and job openings. A formal relationship could also enhance the labor exchange's abilities to serve job-seekers, as it now seeks to do, such as by providing projections of the fields in which job opportunities will develop.

CHAPTER THREE

Improving Technical and Vocational Education and Training in the KRI

The KRI is enjoying rapid economic growth, creating many new jobs. Many of these jobs require a solid education and technical skills. The ability of the KRI and its government to provide needed skills to the labor force will help to determine how rapidly the region's economy will grow.

Over the past few years, the KRG has launched an ambitious reform of basic and secondary education and has expanded opportunities for tertiary technical and university education (Vernez, Culbertson, and Constant, 2012). However, secondary-level vocational education has lagged, leaving many students who cannot or do not want to pursue postsecondary education without the necessary skills that would enable them to contribute to the KRI's evolving labor market and economy.

Enrollment in KRI's secondary vocational education has diminished in recent years, and graduates often have difficulty finding employment. Unemployment among youth (aged 15 to 24) is currently 18 percent. At the same time, employers complain that graduates from local general and vocational educational institutions do not possess the skills they need, including numeracy, writing, information technology, and hands-on technical skills. In response, firms are said to resort to hiring foreign labor whenever they cannot find local graduates with the right skills.

As part of its sweeping efforts to transform and grow the KRI's education system, the KRG asked RAND to assess its technical and vocational education and training system and to offer strategic recommendations for enabling it to better meet the needs of both labor markets and students. We undertook several tasks, including a literature review on effective TVET systems, analyses of secondary data on TVET programs in the KRI, interviews with leaders and staff of the KRI ministries responsible for TVET, case studies of TVET systems in other countries, and a survey of KRI employers on their workforce needs.

The KRI Offers Three Types of Vocational Education

The current TVET system has secondary, postsecondary, and adult components, each administered by a different government ministry. Three ministries provide TVET, targeting different populations of students:

- The MOE offers secondary students (grades 10 through 12) *vocational education* (ISCED 3).[1] The 32 secondary-level vocational schools enrolled 8,600 students in 2011–12, or 3 percent of all secondary-school students.
- The MOHESR provides *technical education* in 23 two-year *technical institutes* and two four-year *technical colleges* to graduates from secondary schools. These schools enrolled about 30,000 students in 2012, accounting for 33 percent of postsecondary students.
- The Ministry of Labor and Social Affairs (MOLSA) provides *vocational skills* training in three training centers to adults aged 18 or older who did not complete compulsory basic education (that is, education through grade 9) or who want to obtain some professional training. Less than 1 percent of adults each year participate in such training.

Figure 3.1 illustrates the flow of students (moving from the bottom level upward) through the various components of the TVET and general education system of the KRI, using the cohort of students who completed basic education in 2007 and who are expected to complete four years of university in 2014. We derived the number of students at each stage by following the basic-education graduating class of 2007 (that is, students who completed 9th grade that

Figure 3.1
Progression of Students Through the TVET and Education System: Cohort That Graduated from Basic Education in 2007

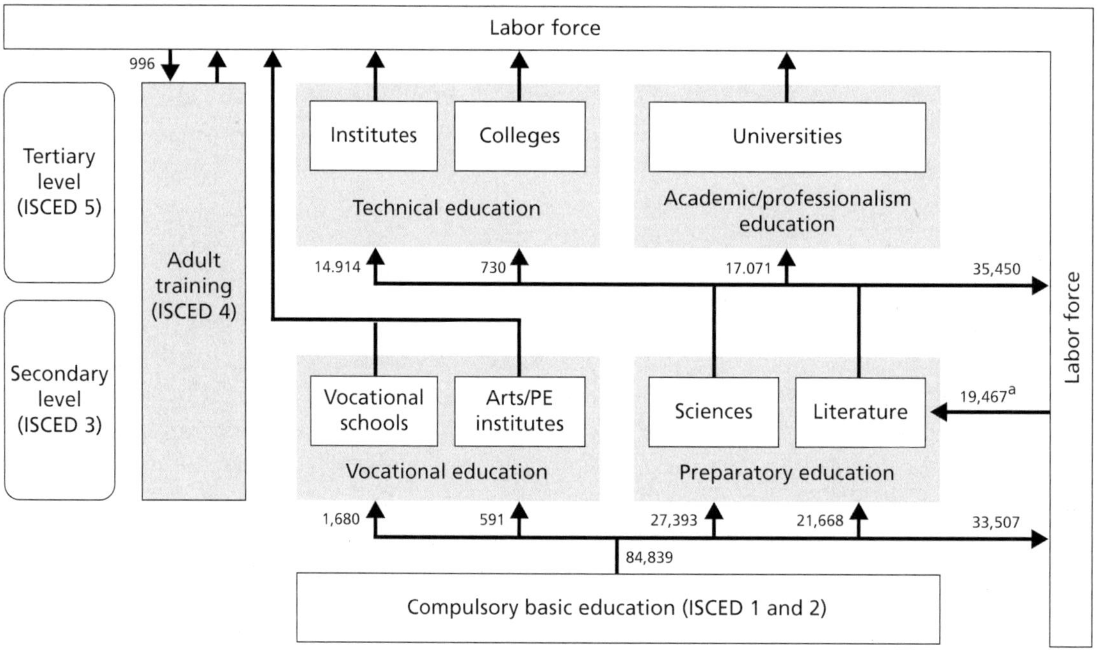

[a]These are individuals who had left schools and eventually returned to complete their secondary education.
SOURCES: MOE, MOHESR, and MOLSA.
RAND *RR873 3.1*

---

[1] The International Standard Classification of Education (ISCED) is a classification for organizing information on education and training by UNESCO. It is used for assembling, compiling, and presenting statistics both within countries and internationally (UNESCO, 2006). We use this classification of educational levels for those readers who are most familiar with it as well as the terminology more commonly used in the KRI.

year) through subsequent years until 2011. The number of students progressing through each level of education may vary by cohort.

The bottom of the figure shows that 84,839 students completed compulsory basic education in 2007. Of these, most (58 percent) went on to secondary preparatory schools, 3 percent went on to vocational education and arts/physical education institutes, and the remainder (39 percent) left the education system. Of the students leaving the education system after completing basic education, many later returned and completed their secondary education.

All students who attended secondary vocational education left the education system (with many entering the labor force) upon completing these programs of study. Of the students who graduated from secondary education in 2010, more than half (52 percent) did not continue with their studies, while 23 percent matriculated at a tertiary technical education institute or college and the remaining 25 percent went on to academic or professional education at a university. Only about 1,000 adults completed training in an adult training center in 2010.

These data indicate the following:

- The share of secondary students choosing vocational education (4 percent) was low, while the share of postsecondary students assigned to tertiary technical education was relatively high (48 percent).
- A sizable share of basic-education graduates (39 percent) and of secondary preparatory education graduates (52 percent) did not continue their studies to the next level but instead left the education system and may have joined the labor force.
- Overall, some 70,000 students yearly may be joining the labor market annually without having received any specific preparation for employment.
- There is no pathway for graduates from secondary vocational schools to continue on to tertiary education, either technical or academic.

Enrollment in Tertiary Technical Schools Is Growing, While Enrollment in Secondary Vocational Schools Is Low

Over the past five years, enrollment trends in the KRI have differed sharply between secondary vocational and tertiary technical education (Figure 3.2). Student enrollment in secondary vocational education diminished by one-half from 2006–07 to 2007–08, and although it increased slightly in subsequent years, it has not yet regained its previous higher level. By contrast, enrollment in technical institutes and colleges more than quadrupled between 2006–07 and 2010–11. Today, about 50 percent of tertiary students graduate with a technical diploma, up from 27 percent in 2007. In part to accommodate this growth, five new technical institutes have opened since 2006.

There are many reasons for the low enrollment in secondary vocational education, including a strong cultural bias against secondary vocational education, outdated curricula, the inability of most graduates to find jobs, and the inability for students to matriculate from secondary-level TVET to postsecondary education. Only a small percentage of TVET graduates (estimated at 10 to 20 percent) can find jobs, while academic secondary school and university are viewed as more prestigious.

Figure 3.2
Student Enrollment Trends in Secondary Vocational and Tertiary Technical Education, 2007–2012

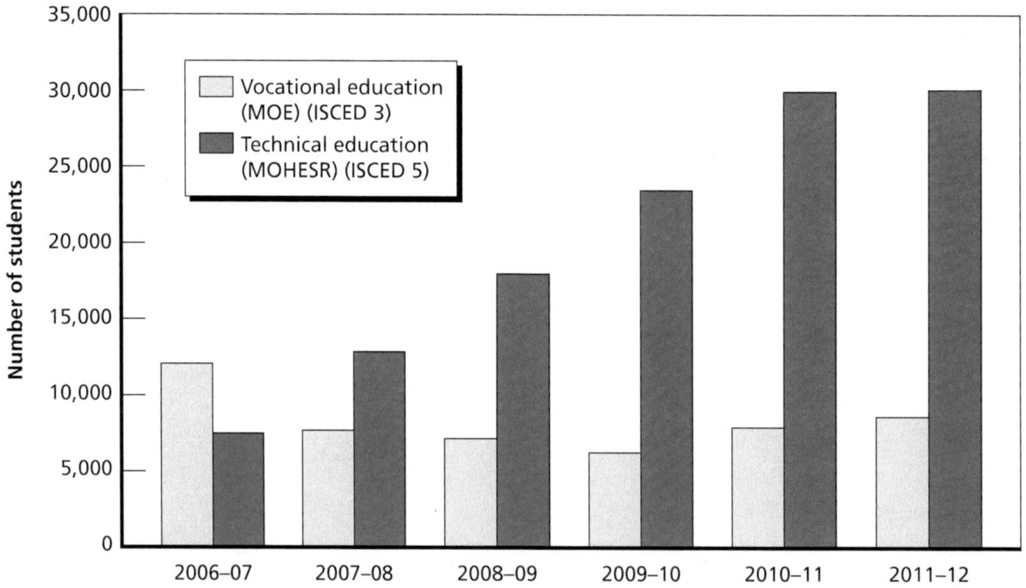

SOURCES: MOE and MOHESR.
RAND *RR873-3.2*

The KRI's Current TVET Preparation Does Not Meet the Needs of the Labor Market or Students

There are challenges facing TVET in the KRI. Most TVET curricula are reportedly 10 to 20 years old, or even older. Staff at all three ministries said they are planning to revise their curricula, and some work has started toward this goal. Still, much remains to be done on a continuing basis to increase and institutionalize the local capacity to revise and develop curricula. New curricula also will require upgrading the preparation of thousands of teachers. Teachers also may need retraining as workshop equipment is modernized.

There is also very little coordination between TVET providers and the labor market, in particular, the private sector. Perhaps one of the most important challenges will be developing an institutionalized relationship between TVET providers and the private sector. This partnership will be important for

- matching the type of and enrollment in TVET occupational training to the evolving occupational demand of the economy
- upgrading occupational standards and the curricula to incorporate the skills desired by employers
- increasing the opportunities for on-the-job training.

Currently, student assignment to TVET occupations depends more on institutional supply than on labor-market demand. The number and mix of occupational programs has remained mostly unchanged over time and is insufficiently diverse, especially in secondary vocational schools and MOLSA's training centers. Although TVET curricula specify a two-month internship in the government or private sector, it is not necessarily related to the students' area of studies and lacks quality assurance. Nevertheless, one reform planned for tertiary TVET is to increase on-the-job training to six months in the two-year programs and one year for the four-year programs. This makes it even more crucial to start developing partnerships with employers.

TVET governance also needs attention. It is currently divided among three ministries with separate policy and operational control. There is little coordination across the ministries responsible for TVET, so the curricula are not aligned among the different levels. Ideally, the secondary vocational education and tertiary technical education curricula should be aligned so that students can advance from lower to higher levels and have the opportunity to gain increasingly complex knowledge and skills in the same occupational area.

TVET Can Help Graduates Prepare for Current and Future Jobs

The KRI's education and training institutions require systematic information about the demand for employees and skills in order to set occupational standards, determine what occupational programs to offer, determine the level of student enrollment desirable, and design curricula. We used data from the 2012 KRLFS to analyze current employment patterns in the KRI and to gain a full picture of where jobs are concentrated and how that matches up to the supply of secondary versus postsecondary TVET graduates. We also collected data and assessed the work-readiness of the local labor force as perceived by employers, to identify the skills gaps that need to be addressed, and assessed employer demands for skills to inform our recommendations for improving the alignment of TVET provision with labor-market needs.

Expected employment growth in the KRI economy is likely to be largely in the service, wholesale, and transportation sectors—and individuals with a secondary-level vocational education could fill many of these jobs. Nearly three-fourths of jobs in the private sector are in occupations—services and sales, skilled agricultural, craft and related trades, plant, machine operators and assemblers, and clerical support positions—for which secondary vocational education and training may provide adequate preparation.

We asked employers about the work readiness of graduates from KRI education and TVET institutions. About 40 percent of employers said that graduates from secondary schools were poorly or very poorly prepared for work, and a smaller share (25 percent) said that graduates from tertiary institutions—both technical institutes and universities—are poorly or very poorly prepared for work (Figure 3.3). Also, 25 percent of employers said they had difficulties filling positions that required a secondary education.

The most common shortcomings employers encountered with TVET graduates include

- lack of prior work experience, cited by 40 percent of employers
- lack of educational qualifications for the job (31 percent)
- lack of appropriate skills (21 percent).

A large share of employers reported hiring employees from outside the KRI. The average share of employees from elsewhere across surveyed employers was 17 percent. Larger employers were significantly more likely than both small and medium-sized employers to have employees from outside the KRI. The average shares of employees not from the KRI in both mining and

Figure 3.3
Percentage of Employers, by How Well Prepared for Work Local Graduates Are and Level of Education, 2012

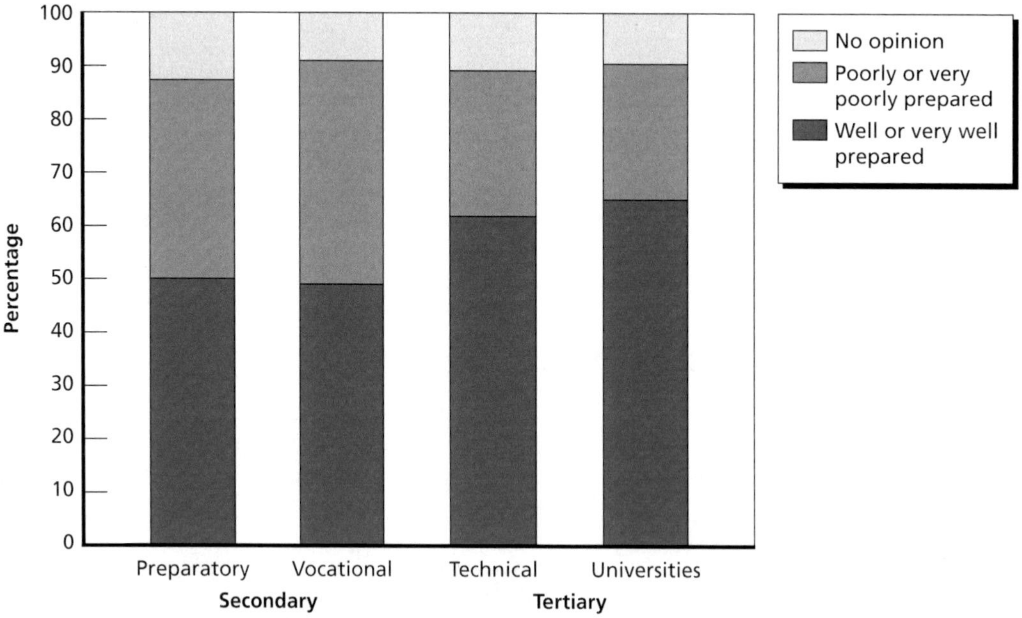

SOURCE: RAND Survey of Business Establishments (2012).
NOTE: N = 360. The survey question was, "How prepared for work are graduates from <type of school> within the Kurdistan Region of Iraq?"
RAND *RR873-3.3*

manufacturing and infrastructure were significantly larger than in the services and professions (e.g., wholesale and retail trade, tourism, real estate, and financial services).

Employers identified a lack of experience and of appropriate technical skills as major barriers to hiring locally. Other skill deficits included foreign languages and use of information technology, as well as "soft skills" such as communication, dealing with customers, and teamwork. Occupations for which employers had particular difficulties hiring included technicians, process plant and machine operators, sales and customer service, and some skilled trades.

International Practices Provide Lessons for Improving TVET in the KRI

The KRI is not unique in its need to develop TVET programs. Several countries have developed such successful programs and use them to develop their workforces, provide graduates with skills, and meet other societal goals. Our country case studies (Germany, Finland, Jordan, Korea, Tunisia, and Turkey) and international literature on TVET systems and programs identified many practices that provide lessons for improving TVET in the KRI.

TVET systems and education systems in general have several components, including

- governance
- involvement of employers and other social partners
- finance

- occupational offerings
- occupational demand and skill forecasting
- delivery methods
- curriculum
- student admission, progression, and graduation requirements
- guidance and counseling
- teacher and trainer qualifications
- quality assurance

We discuss a few of these below.

Governance. The governance system sets forth the division of TVET's responsibilities at various levels—national, regional, and local entities—and the legal framework under which TVET is provided. In the KRI, governance of secondary vocational education is entrusted to the MOE, while the MOHESR oversees tertiary technical education, and the MOLSA has oversight of adult technical education. There is little collaboration among these three levels. Most countries have TVET responsibilities defined by law, and most are moving toward more coordination among stakeholders (e.g., government agencies, different levels of government, and social partners such as employer bodies, trade unions, student unions). Two main governance models are used for TVET: a centralized model in which authority for TVET lies with one ministry (Jordan), and a decentralized model in which several ministries and levels of government share authority for TVET, with some level of coordination across organizations (Korea, Tunisia, Turkey, Finland, and Germany).

Involvement of Employers and Other Social Partners. The involvement of social partners (employers, sector bodies, trade unions, student unions) is considered crucial to ensuring the labor-market relevance of TVET programs. Social partners' participation is legislated in some countries, which in effect gives them a formal role in TVET governance. In the KRI, there are no institutional mechanisms to engage the participation of social partners in TVET. Other nations, however, have several such mechanisms. In Finland, for instance, social partners participate through National Tripartite Committees for each occupational field, with a responsibility to plan and develop vocational requirements. Jordan's employment and technical and vocational education and training council enables industry, trade unions, and training providers to play a role in TVET. Turkey has National and Provincial Education Boards to advise on curriculum.

Finance. Typically, TVET systems either are fully funded by the public, as in the KRI, or partially funded by the public, with varying levels of contributions by employers or students. TVET is fully funded by the public in Finland (42 percent national and 58 percent local); in Jordan, 85 percent is publicly funded. In Germany, financing of secondary vocational programs is based on a system of mixed public and private financing.

Curriculum. Most countries' secondary vocational programs include literacy and numeracy requirements. In addition to technical skills, many also aim to develop the soft skills that employers want, such as an ability to work in teams, communicate with customers, and think critically. The duration of secondary vocational education ranges from one to two years in Jordan and Tunisia to four years in Switzerland and Turkey. In the KRI, secondary vocational programs are three years in duration, and the teaching of soft skills is not included in the current curriculum.

Occupational Offerings. All TVET systems need mechanisms to balance student preferences for TVET and labor-market needs. The KRI offers only 14 occupational options in secondary vocational education, while most countries offer more than 100 occupations (Table 3.1). Occupations can include construction trades, transportation, commerce and administration, healthcare, agriculture, design, energy, food preparation, accounting, tourism, and personal services.

Occupational Demand and Skills Forecasting. Although the KRI has no formal or informal process to assess labor-market needs and determine the number and content of occupational programs, other countries use a variety of such tools. These include surveys of employers and recent graduates and projections of future occupational and qualifications requirements. The information generated is necessary to determine the kinds of occupational training to provide, help make changes in training curricula, guide the choices students make, and otherwise determine desirable improvements in TVET policy and practices.

Student Counseling and Guidance. Although the KRI provides no counseling and guidance services to students, student counseling and guidance is considered a key component of other countries' TVET systems, especially as careers diversify. While some countries (Jordan, Korea) have no or weak counseling and guidance systems, several others (Austria, Finland, Switzerland) integrate guidance into the curriculum at all levels of education from primary to tertiary and adult education. In Switzerland, career guidance is formally scheduled during the time of early compulsory education.

Table 3.1
Percentage of Students in Secondary Vocational Education and Number of Occupational Offerings in Selected Countries, 2010

Country	Number of Occupational Offerings	Percentage of Students in Secondary Vocational Education (ISCED 3)
Germany	349	58
Switzerland	250	64
Austria	245	72
Jordan	200	12
Turkey	197	64
Finland	187	71
Tunisia	150	11
Norway	112	50
KRI	14	3

SOURCES: Cedefop, 2012; Eurobarometer, 2011.

Recommendations for Improving TVET

The findings suggest several recommendations for improving TVET in the KRI, particularly at the secondary level.

Establish governance structure, objectives, and legislation for TVET. We recommend that the KRI establish a TVET Governing Council to coordinate policy and support and sustain improvement. This council would include representatives from all relevant ministries and the governorates, as well as Occupation Committees with representation from employers, trade unions, teachers, and other social partners. The TVET Governing Council would have the authority to coordinate policymaking and develop a TVET vision, objectives, and overall strategy. An example of a proposed governance structure is shown in Figure 3.4.

Having information about market needs and trends will be important for the MOE when designing the three new secondary vocational centers and selecting new occupational programs. We recommend that the MOE begin collecting data about market signals as an early priority.

Enact TVET legislation. It will eventually be desirable for the KRG to enact legislation formalizing the TVET governance structure, granting it the appropriate authority, and defining the division of responsibilities among government, employers, and other social partners. Nearly all TVET systems have their governance, main features, and requirements coded into law to provide clarity and direction to stakeholders.

Increase vocational education participation to 20 percent of secondary students. The KRG is planning a threefold increase in participation of secondary students in vocational education, with the three planned centers offering as many as 10,000 spaces each. The MOE

Figure 3.4
Proposed TVET Governance Structure

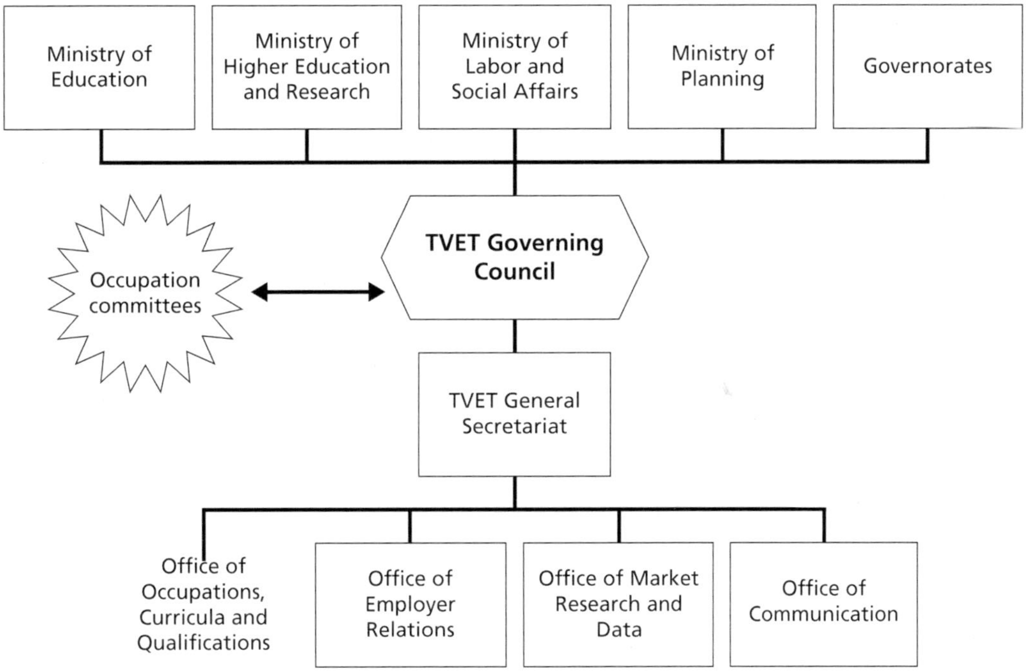

RAND *RR873-3.4*

also may set a goal for 20 percent of the secondary-school-age population to participate in vocational education over the next ten years, with further increases after that. We endorse this goal. Increasing participation would provide sufficient preparation for about 70 percent of KRI jobs, would provide TVET graduates with marketable skills without having to complete postsecondary education, and would provide an initial foundation of technical skills and knowledge so that tertiary technical education could focus on providing more advanced and specialized skills.

Develop occupation standards and set student qualification requirements. We recommend that the KRI develop occupation-specific and group-of-occupations standards that set new, more rigorous credentials for occupations offered through secondary, tertiary, and adult education, with diplomas offered at different skill levels. The standards should be consistent across the KRI and designed by the Occupation Committees.

Upgrade the secondary vocational education curriculum. To improve students' numeracy and language skills, we recommend broadening the curriculum content for the academic subjects of the secondary vocational education program so that they are the same as for the preparatory program. The teaching of soft skills—such as teamwork, interpersonal skills, critical thinking and problem solving, ability to work independently, time management, responsibility, work ethic, and handling of customers—could be added to the curriculum for many occupational offerings. Similarly, training in the use of information and computer technology applications could be added to the general subjects of selected occupational offerings.

KRI employers say that they would like TVET graduates to have more practical workplace experience than they do currently. Students may gain such experience through workshop-based programs, workplace internships, or apprenticeship programs. In school-based programs, such as in the three new secondary vocational centers or in other TVET facilities, workshops could be designed to simulate the workplace environment. Although the KRI's TVET programs already require internships at the secondary and tertiary levels, they need to be more formally defined for both students and employers in order to be effective and ensure quality. We also recommend undertaking pilot programs in which apprentices receive most of their training at a company.

Coordinate progression from secondary and tertiary TVET programs. As curricula are developed for secondary vocational schools, it will be necessary to revise technical education curricula offered at tertiary technical institutes to ensure that they are of sufficient breadth and depth for students to progress to higher technician levels. The TVET Governing Council and Secretariat should coordinate the student-progression process from level to level, ensuring that students receiving diplomas from secondary vocational education have the skills needed to continue.

Expand occupational programs. Expanding the range of occupational programs not only would broaden the appeal of secondary vocational education to KRI students but would make the system more responsive to the labor market. We recommend increasing the number of programs over the next ten years, based on assessments of market demand. As a starting point, we recommend that the MOE consult with the largest employers in the KRI and establish programs to meet their needs.

Set additional teacher preparation requirements and create plans to develop enough qualified teachers. It will be especially important for vocational teachers and trainers to have relevant occupational qualifications and experience. In addition, the KRI will need a large number of new teachers to staff the three planned new vocational centers. The new secondary vocational centers could provide opportunities for current teachers of vocational subjects to gain up-to-date, practical experience in workplaces. New requirements should also be set for new teachers, both general and vocational. Teachers in the general subjects in the vocational program should have the same academic qualifications as general teachers in the secondary preparatory schools.

Establish offices at TVET providers to provide student counseling and guidance. Students should receive guidance and counseling. As a starting point, we recommend setting up guidance offices at the three new secondary vocational facilities and at the technical education institutes. These offices should employ counselors who are experienced in labor-market issues and who can call on a wide range of information to support students at key career-decision points.

Conclusion

Implementing these recommendations can help the KRI support its rapid economic growth through a vocational education and training system that would better align with its needs and also reflect international best practices.

CHAPTER FOUR

Health Sector Reform in the KRI

The KRG asked RAND to help guide reform of the health care system in the KRI. The overarching goal of reform was to establish a health system that would provide high-quality services efficiently to everyone to prevent, treat, and manage physical and mental illnesses and injuries. In the first phase of our work, we focused on (1) primary care, (2) projecting health care demand and utilization, and (3) laying out the principles of health finance reform. This section summarizes the second phase of RAND's work.

In Phase II of the study, we analyzed three distinct but intertwined health policy issue areas: financing policy development, implementation of early primary care recommendations, and quality and patient safety assessment and recommendations. These were selected by the KRG's Minister of Health and the Minister of Planning as areas of particular concern as it continues to improve its health care system. At the request of the ministers, we examined each issue, reviewed the relevant literature, explored the issue in discussions with key stakeholders, developed and assessed various policy options, and developed plans or approaches to overcome barriers and achieve stated policy objectives. In the area of primary care, we also developed and helped to implement a new management information system.

There Are Challenges to Implementing Health Financing Reform in the KRI

The way a country finances its health care system is fundamental to the country's ability to meet its national health objectives. The KRG asked RAND to examine the current health care financing system and to develop options and a strategic roadmap to help guide reform efforts.

A health financing system must address five fundamental issues about care, as shown in Figure 4.1.

In the KRI, the draft KRG constitution makes it clear that all KRI residents have a right to, or are eligible for, basic health care services provided in the public sector, although exactly what services are covered (the benefits package) has never been defined. Funding for public-sector health services comes primarily from the KRG budget, which is funded mostly by a 17-percent allocation from the Iraqi budget, while private-sector care is paid for by individuals in cash.

Pooling of funds to spread risk occurs in the KRG budget, which provides budget allocations to providers, such as hospitals and primary health care centers (PHCs), and pays staff salaries. The way in which services are purchased ideally provides incentives to purchase the *right amount* of the *right kind* of services; however, currently in the KRI, such incentives are lacking. Physicians are paid a salary by the Ministry of Finance (MOF), and facilities receive

Figure 4.1
Basic Elements of Health Care Financing

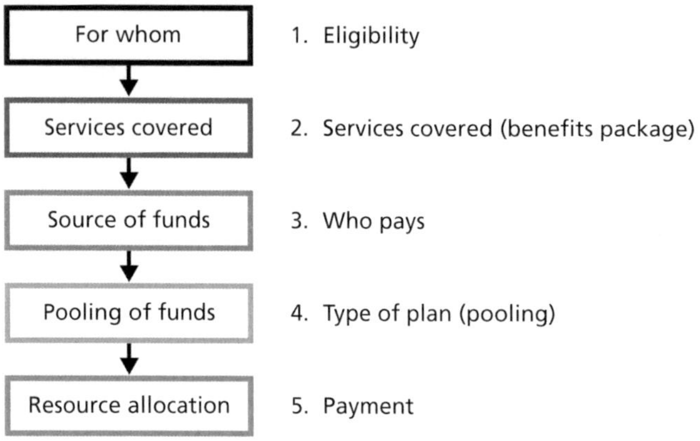

RAND *RR873-4.1*

a budget. There is no relationship between pay and performance: The system does not reward facilities that do a good job or physicians who work longer hours and provide more care in the public sector.

The private sector is estimated to account for 20 to 30 percent of health care spending. A substantial amount of this care is provided by physicians who are paid salaries in the public sector but spend significant amounts of time working in private-sector clinics, where pay is higher. This phenomenon is often referred to as *dual practice.*

To move forward with health financing reform, KRG policymakers will need to overcome a number of challenges:

- **Insufficient funding:** Resources are insufficient—particularly in the public system—to adequately meet the current demand for health care, and the situation will worsen as the population grows and incomes increase.
- **Perception that health care should be free:** In the proposed constitution, it is clear that the KRG believes that health care is a basic public right, and the government is committed to providing a basic package of care to all KRI residents. Because that care has been provided thus far with very minimal out-of-pocket costs to the public, people have come to believe that they are entitled to free care from the public sector, an entitlement that would not be sustainable in the long run.
- **Lack of data and information systems:** The data needed to make good management decisions, set financing policy, and manage a modern financing system are not currently available in the KRI.
- **Inadequate organizational capacity in the Ministry of Health (MOH):** The MOH does not currently have the capacity, personnel, or funding required to implement or manage envisioned health care financing reform.
- **Small co-payments:** Patient co-payments in the public sector are too low to raise funds or provide incentives for appropriate use.
- **Physical state of hospital facilities:** The hospital sector is hampered by the need for renovation and modern equipment because of Saddam-era neglect, and hospital admin-

istrators have little control over staffing and minimal budget flexibility. Most hospital administrators are respected doctors with little or no management training.
- **Inappropriate incentives:** The health financing system provides no incentives to reward work, performance, or productivity. This is particularly true among doctors whose salaries do not reflect the amount or quality of public-sector service they provide.
- **Unguided growth of private-sector health care:** The private sector is rapidly expanding without regulatory guidance or a strategic investment process.

Because of these challenges, this is a good time for the KRG to make key decisions about the future of its health care system. The country has significant resources to support its aspirations. The lack of an entrenched system presents an opportunity to develop and implement a strategic health care vision that improves the availability of high-quality care and provides it more cost-effectively.

A Strategic Vision and Road Map for Health Financing Reform

RAND developed a strategic vision and road map to guide health financing reform in the KRI over the next decade. The road map lays out a two-phase approach to achieve the aims of the strategy. The focus for the next five to seven years should be on Phase I; whether the KRG decides to move to Phase II will depend on many factors that are years in the future.

Phase I, to be fully implemented over the next five to seven years, envisions moving from the present budget-funded system to an efficient and effective Accountable National Health Service (A-NHS). The government would be responsible for funding for health care and continue to be responsible for providing services for all citizens except for those who opt voluntarily to use the private sector; however, revenue collection, incentives, and managerial responsibility would differ significantly from the status quo. The resulting system would provide better care, more clearly meet residents' needs, and encourage productivity and incorporate incentives for efficiency and constant quality improvement.

As part of the movement to an A-NHS, the overall package of benefits provided by the public health system would be defined and clarified to be comprehensive but also limited by the resources available and the policy choices of leaders. A wage tax to help fund a national health insurance pool would be phased in, and incentives would be realigned to encourage efficiency and quality on the part of hospitals and doctors. At the end of Phase I, hospitals would be independent cost centers that control their own budgets, and new rules and incentives concerning physicians working in both the public and private sectors will have been put into place. A new agency—either part of the MOH or independent of it—would manage a health insurance fund and collect contributions from the central government and distribute them to service providers. Moving to a well-functioning A-NHS is an ambitious undertaking that will require the focus of the KRG for the foreseeable future.

In Phase II, the KRG should consider whether to move to a functioning social health insurance (SHI) system along with an organizational structure to manage the system. Everyone would be expected to obtain insurance coverage. The SHI system would process and pay claims based on a payment model that encourages efficiency and increases productivity. If the KRG makes the choice to move to an SHI, the insurance fund would pay for services that could be provided in either public or private care facilities.

The phases and major components of the health care financing strategy are shown in Figure 4.2.

Prerequisites and Policy Actions for Implementing Financing Reform

RAND identified prerequisites, as well as policy actions, needed in each phase to achieve the established objectives. Prerequisites and policy actions for Phase I are shown in Table 4.1.

Phase I prerequisites of change include improved data systems, a modernized MOH, improvements in the quality of care in the public sector, issuance of health cards, and establishment of an organizational structure to manage the new system.

Phase I policy actions include encouraging the growth of private insurance to create needed skills, such as claim processing and payment, setting benefits packages, paying providers, evaluating risk and new technologies, and collecting and using data to guide business practices. A wage tax would be imposed on salaried employees working in government service or for large firms. Employers of foreign workers would be required to pay the full actuarial costs of their insurance. Other policy actions include explicitly defining the package of publicly supplied health benefits to which the government obligates itself, hospital-sector reform, and policy changes related to physicians who practice in both the public and private sectors.

Figure 4.2
Two-Phase Health Care Financing Strategy

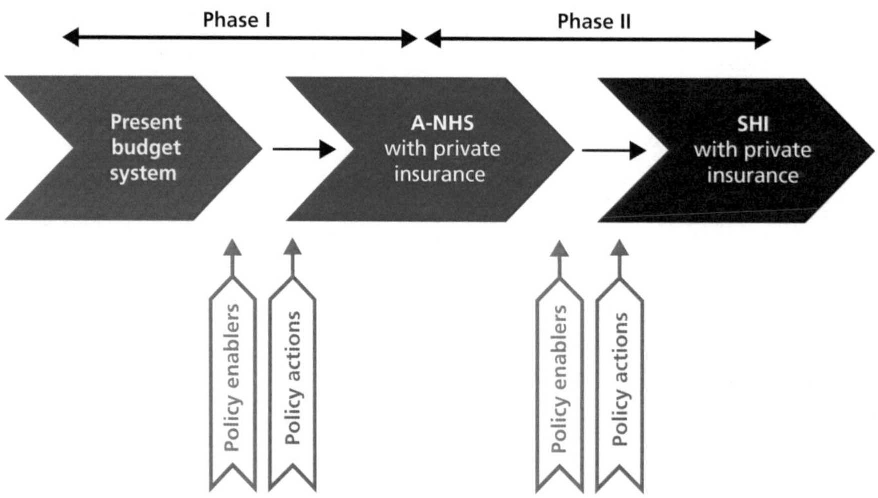

RAND *RR873-4.2*

Table 4.1
Prerequisites and Policy Actions for Phase I

Prerequisites	Policy Actions
1. Develop data system and conduct analysis	1. Define benefits package
2. Modernize MOH	2. Introduce private insurance
3. Gain political approval and funding	3. Deal with physician dual-practice issue
4. Implement hospital and physician licensure	4. Implement hospital structure reform
5. Issue individual insurance cards	5. Introduce health insurance wage tax
6. Establish and provide hospital management training	6. Require expatriates to pay full cost

Once a fully functioning A-NHS has been well established (over five to seven years), the KRG may wish to move to Phase II and adopt an SHI system with supplemental private insurance to fund public health care in the KRI. Phase II prerequisites and policy actions are shown in Table 4.2.

Phase II prerequisites include enhancing the KRG's ability to levy and collect taxes, synchronizing policy with Baghdad, and establishing a new Social Insurance Agency, which would be responsible for developing payment policies, processing claims, and paying providers for the services they render.

Phase II policy actions include introducing an SHI system, building on the structure to manage the system developed in Phase I. In collaboration with the MOF, the new agency would set wage tax rates and SHI rates; the KRG may choose to subsidize some groups and develop a system to provide care for the poor.

Supplemental private insurance would be allowed in both phases to supplement payment for uncovered or partially covered services in the public sector and to help individuals spread their risk should they decide to use the private sector. People would still be required to support the public system fully even if they choose to purchase supplemental insurance. We would not recommend the adoption of a policy that allows for replacement insurance, in which private insurance is allowed to replace purchase of public insurance, because this almost always leads to two-tiered health care and lower quality in the public system.

Addressing the Dual-Practice Challenge

The term *dual practice* refers to the current practice in the KRI in which physicians, who are paid a salary by the MOF to practice in the public health sector, spend significant amounts of time working in private-sector clinics, where pay is higher. Physicians are also guaranteed a pension whose sum is not related to the quality or quantity of care they provide. After a detailed assessment, RAND concluded that dual practice in KRI was inefficient and costly. It robs the public sector of the manpower it needs to fulfill its obligations, and is ultimately a significant barrier to overall financing and hospital reform.

We identified policy options for addressing the challenges associated with dual practice and examined options from a number of perspectives, including effects on the supply of physicians in the public sector, ease of implementing new policies, regulatory complexity, quality of care, efficiency, and equity. After presenting the ramifications of alternative policies, we recommend an approach to begin to address the dual-practice issue immediately—specifically, by

- requiring physicians to work for three to five years in the public health sector before working in the private sector
- linking wages to number of hours worked
- reforming physician pensions to link payouts to years of service.

Table 4.2
Prerequisites and Policy Actions for Phase II

Prerequisites	Policy Actions
1. Develop a modern functioning tax system	1. Introduce SHI agency
2. Synchronize policy with Baghdad	2. Set wage-tax rates
3. Ensure an adequate supply of PHCs, hospitals, and trained medical personnel	3. Determine policy to provide for the poor
4. Establish SHI agency	4. Set payment rates

In the longer run, when better data systems are operational and hospital reform is complete, quality of care or procedures performed could be incorporated as measures so that a comprehensive pay-for-performance policy could be established.

Improving Primary Care

In the area of primary care, RAND built on its extensive research and experience in the KRI to begin implementing change. To establish relevant targets and benchmarks, we first analyzed the current health care system in the KRI. The analysis identified many strengths of the existing system, including excellent access to care, an adequate number of health facilities, and knowledgeable and committed providers and leaders. However, the health system also faces challenges. The overall distribution of PHCs and medical staff in the KRI is not optimal. Using Duhok as an example, we found that population coverage by health centers varies widely by governorate and district (Figure 4.3). A main PHC should, in principle, cover no more than 10,000 persons.

Further, the services offered at each type of facility and reporting requirements are not standardized. For example, most main PHCs in Duhok provide vaccinations, but very few branches or sub-centers do so (Figure 4.4), and many PHCs lack key laboratory and X-ray equipment.

To address these issues, we drew on our earlier research and experience to define primary care targets and benchmarks: recommended staffing, equipment, and a suggested list of services that we proposed should be available at each type of health center, from branches/sub-center to main PHCs and family health centers. These recommendations were vetted among health policy leaders in the KRI before being finalized. The Minister of Health accepted these as the new policy of the MOH, translated the document RAND developed into Kurdish, and disseminated it to the Directors General of all governorates to use as their planning targets.

To support implementation of the policy, we developed a management information system (MIS) so that the MOH could determine which health centers have the specified staffing and equipment and are providing the expected services. The MIS provides a wide range of information for ongoing planning and management at all levels across the KRI. A screenshot of the MIS menu page is shown in Figure 4.5.

We developed and pilot-tested the data form, revised it based on testing in Duhok and in-depth discussion with representatives from all general directorates, and began to implement it with the assistance of the MOH and Departments of Health (DOHs) in all governorates, and began to implement it with the assistance of the Minister of Health and DOHs in all governorates. The MOH translated the form into Kurdish and sent it to all DOHs for data collection. As of late November 2012, only Duhok had submitted completed data, but data have been collected and are pending from the other governorates.

The Duhok data enable a number of important insights, and a broader range of insights will be possible once the data from Erbil and Sulaimaniya governorates are processed and outputs generated. The data enable the KRG to compare the standards of service with the existing situations, thus giving the MOH and DOHs a powerful tool to help manage primary care and guide policy reform.

Figure 4.3
Population Coverage by KRG Primary Health Care Centers, by Jurisdiction

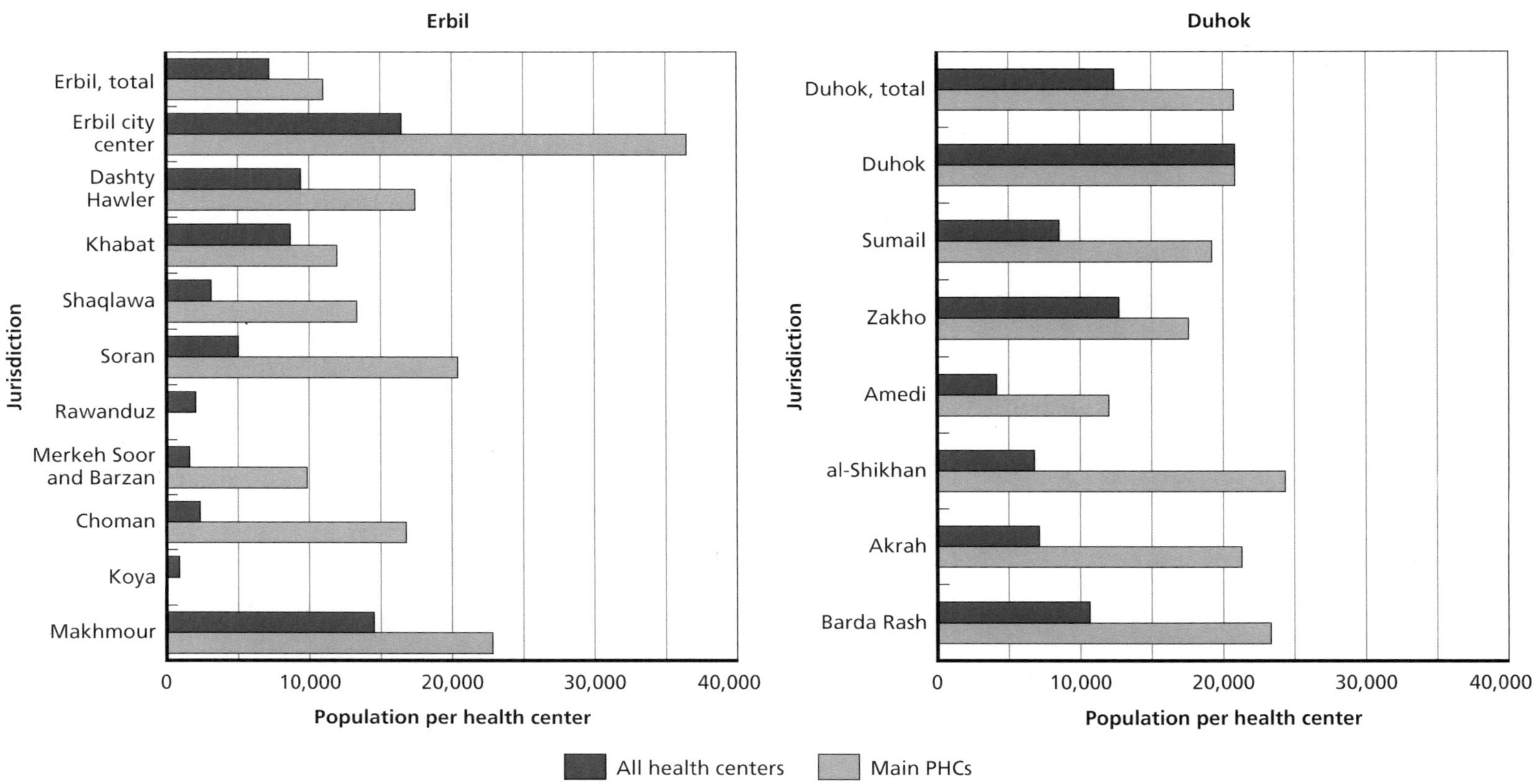

SOURCES: Duhok Department of Health data; Wahab and Petros, 2011.
RAND *RR873-4.3*

Figure 4.4
Health Care Centers Providing Vaccination Services

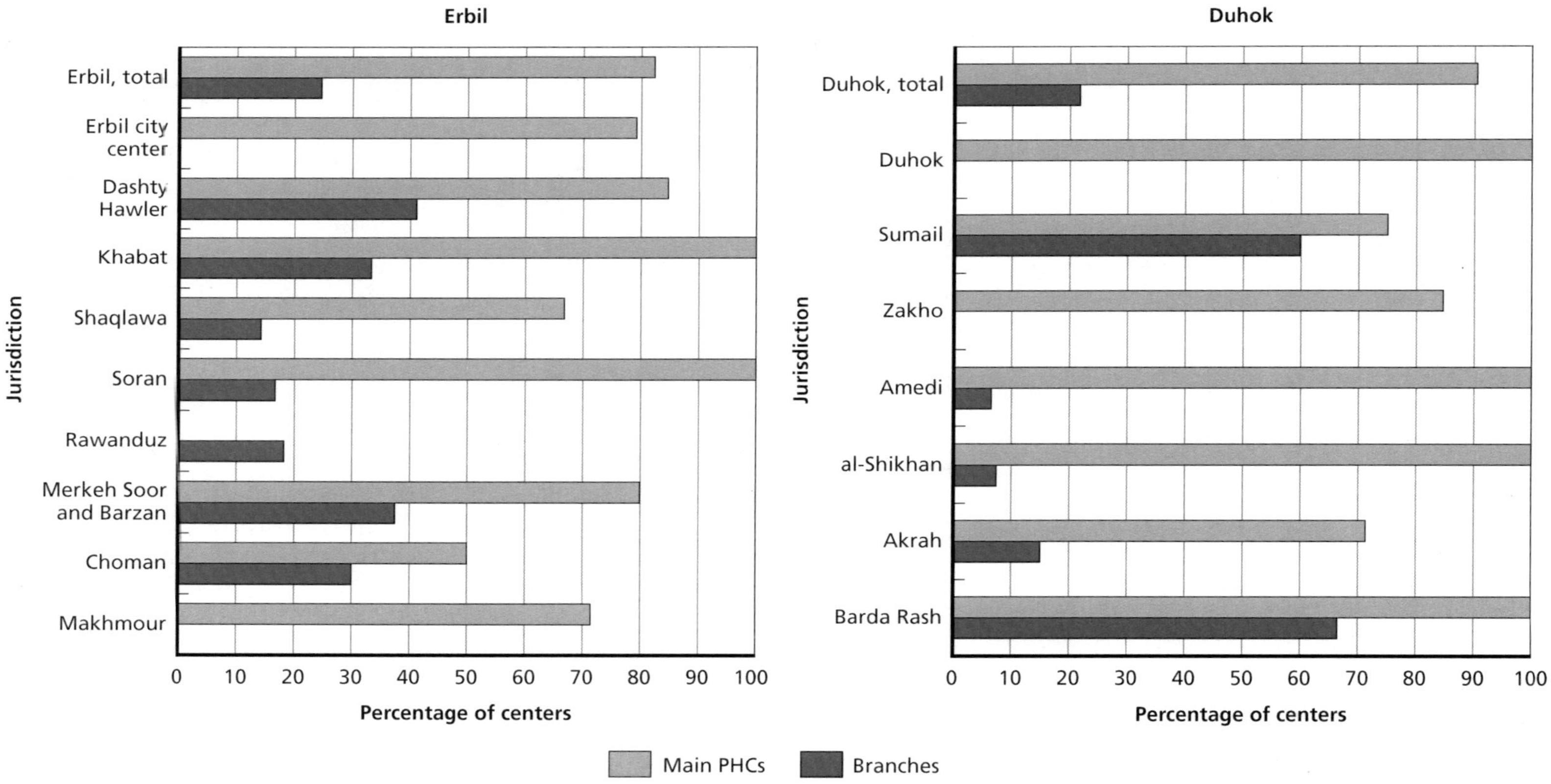

SOURCES: Duhok Department of Health data; Wahab and Petros, 2011.

RAND *RR873-4.4*

Figure 4.5
MIS Menu Page

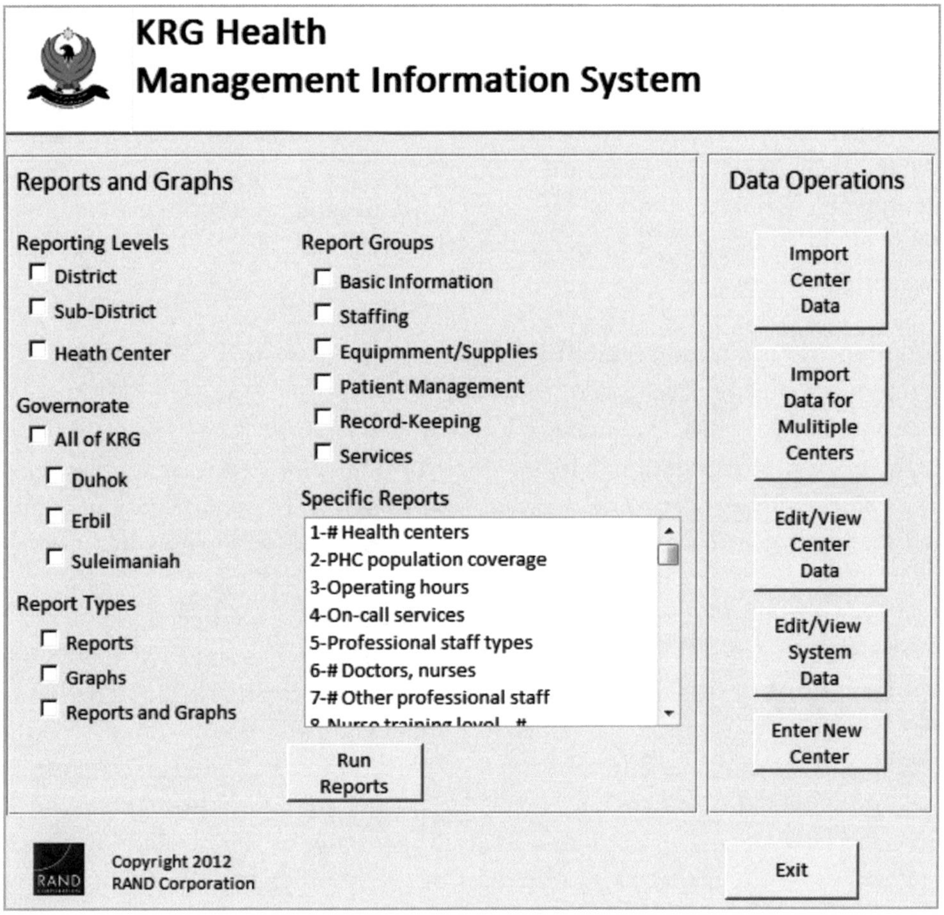

RAND *RR873-4.5*

Improving Patient Safety and Health Care Quality

RAND conducted an initial assessment of patient safety—a vital dimension of overall quality of care—in public hospitals in the KRI. We based our assessment on site visits and discussions with officials, health care managers, and care providers throughout the KRI. We examined patient safety in the context of the landmark framework developed by the U.S. Institute of Medicine.

Initial Findings from RAND's Patient Safety Assessment

An important observation emerging from RAND's assessment was that providers are aware of limitations in their ability to deliver care in the current practice milieu. This realization is key, because the most powerful enabler of change is a cadre of professionals who will be responsible for "owning" the future health care delivery system. The RAND team also learned about specific quality improvement initiatives already under way—for example, at the Azadi Teaching Hospital in Duhok—and about specific legislation designed to protect patient rights.

However, what was lacking was a consistent, organized plan for improving quality and safety across all health care facilities. Most efforts appeared to depend on the initiatives and desires of specific individuals within isolated hospital systems.

Given the current state of health care delivery in the KRI, an explicit assessment against each of the Institute of Medicine goals was not possible. However, some initial specific efforts are beginning in some domains of quality (e.g., safety). By contrast, dual practice, as it exists in the KRI, creates a system that is not equitable for all patients, encourages inefficiencies in the delivery of care, and challenges the combined public and private systems (mostly the public system) when attempting to provide timely care. Because physicians have split loyalties between their public and private practices, the delivery system that exists is more provider-centric than patient-centric.

Recommendations for Improving Patient Safety

Given our findings and input from the MOH and Ministry of Planning (MOP), we recommended four concrete activities to guide the KRI's health care providers toward international standards. The first recommendation, which focuses on achieving accreditation for health care facilities, is a phased activity that could begin now, although full implementation would occur over the next five years. The other three recommendations could be implemented over the next year.

Pursue international accreditation for KRI health care facilities. The KRG should develop an accreditation model for health care facilities that is consistent with internationally recognized standards for health care delivery. Accreditation efforts should begin with hospitals, with later expansion to other health care delivery venues. Of the many accreditation models available worldwide, we suggest using the Joint Commission International accreditation model because it is internationally recognized and has been well received throughout the Middle East. Further, because so many hospitals and health systems in the geographic region have already sought accreditation, there are colleagues in neighboring countries who can serve as resources for the KRI's health care leaders.

The Joint Commission International defines five major "quality essentials" under which standards and guidelines are classified.[1] Based on these, RAND recommended five specific actions to the MOH for pursuing international accreditation:

- *Establish a leadership and accountability team.* Both administrative and clinical leadership are essential, and senior leadership will set the direction for the entire organization.
- *Establish a workforce team to enhance human resource management.* Specifically, the KRG must take responsibility for establishing professional licensure requirements consistent with international standards for education, training, and experience.
- *Establish a safe environment-of-care team.* Requirements for ensuring a safe environment will vary across hospital settings but generally include routine inspection of facilities, guaranteeing availability of safe drinking water and electrical power, and establishing programs to reduce nosocomial infections (that is, infections acquired in hospitals and other health care facilities) and use masks, gloves, and other protections as necessary.

---

1 The five essentials that make up the framework for accreditation are (1) leadership process and accountability, (2) a competent and capable workforce, (3) a safe environment for staff and patients, (4) clinical care of patients, and (5) improvement of quality and safety (Joint Commission International, 2010).

- *Establish a team focused on the clinical care of patients.* Requirements include a reliable process for correctly identifying patients, obtaining informed consent when appropriate, providing laboratory and diagnostic imaging services, ensuring that services are appropriate to patient needs, and educating patients and families to participate in the patient's care.
- *Establish a quality and safety team.* Elements here include an adverse-event reporting system, special attention to high-risk processes and high-risk patients, and a system in which patients and family can voice concerns about quality of care. Other key elements including using appropriate clinical practice guidelines and standards and acknowledging that everyone in an organization is responsible for improving quality.

Examine accredited hospitals to learn how they achieved success. Many hospitals in the region have attained Joint Commission International accreditation. Visits to facilities could help KRI health care leaders understand how hospitals and countries have achieved accreditation and develop a network of colleagues within the region who can provide support and guidance.

Attend a Joint Commission International Practicum program. In a Joint Commission International Practicum program, international and regional health care leaders present a hands-on educational program that solidifies participants' understanding of requirements and strategies for pursing accreditation. We recommend that the team from the KRI include regional government leaders and hospital leadership from two or three hospitals that commit to be the first to work toward accreditation.

Establish a regional leadership team. We recommend the establishment of a KRG Quality Health Council led by the MOH and MOP. The Council would provide important oversight and would include five teams of experts in the content of each of the five quality essentials defined by the Joint Commission International framework. Each team can establish specific goals for hospitals within the KRI and identify unifying programs and concepts to help facilities reach those goals. The chair of each team, or a designee, might be appropriate for participation in the practicum recommended above.

Implementing Policies to Pursue Change

Based on detailed assessments and stakeholder input, RAND has recommended specific, practical, achievable policy reforms in the areas of health care financing, primary care, and patient safety. The set of initiatives we have recommended is ambitious. However, as was clear in RAND's discussions with both the governmental and provider communities, the desire to improve the KRI's health care system is genuine and strong.

If fully adopted, the reforms presented here would have a significant impact on improving health care in the KRI over the next several years. They would also provide powerful incentives that would promote higher quality and great efficiency in health care for all KRI residents.

CHAPTER FIVE

Capacity Building at the Kurdistan Region Statistics Office Through Data Collection

Comprehensive and reliable statistics are crucial for policy development in any region or country. Statistics make it possible to identify the most pressing policy needs, track the progress of policies and initiatives currently in place, and plan for future development. Most importantly, statistics provide the foundation for successful policy planning in many areas. The KRI has been hampered by the lack of such statistics as it aims to improve infrastructure, encourage private-sector development, attract foreign investment, and create sustained economic growth.

In a previous study for the KRG (Berry et al., 2012), RAND

- assessed the KRG's existing institutional arrangements for collecting and sharing data
- assessed the data and information infrastructure currently available in the KRI
- identified the KRG's policy priorities to ensure the collection of relevant data for policymaking
- identified data items that need to be collected for each priority area, highlighting those that are most critical for policymakers at the highest level
- recommended data collection methods and provided a roadmap for implementing recommendations, including the steps needed to build the human-resource capacity within the KRG and the KRSO.

In the study described here, we provided assistance in implementing the recommendations from the previous study. This study's overarching objective has been to assist the central statistical organization of the KRI—the KRSO—and the KRG in building the capacity to undertake the recommended data collection.

RAND worked closely with the KRSO to develop, conduct, and analyze the first round of a labor force survey that will be critical to KRG policymaking. This survey, known as the Kurdistan Labor Force Survey, focuses on the critical indicators of unemployment, labor force participation, and other important indicators for the KRI. It is based on international best practices and standards.

RAND provided overall guidance and training, both analytical and hands-on, for the development and implementation of the survey. Because KRSO staff members were involved in the complete life cycle of the survey—from conception through data collection to policy analysis—and because they were responsible for the final execution and analysis of the surveys, they learned by doing.

The KRI Built Its Data Collection Capacity

The study was carried out in a highly collaborative nature with key staff identified by the KRG, thereby supporting the overall aim of building capacity within the KRG and the KRSO. This capacity-building role is one that RAND has played for many public- and private-sector organizations around the world.

This effort took place over approximately 12 months and included two rounds of an unemployment survey (the first in July 2012, the second in December 2012) and the development of recommendations for an establishment survey that can supply data for calculating the KRI's gross regional product (GRP). The core study tasks included

- design the sampling approach for the KRLFS
- develop the labor force survey questionnaire, working closely with KRSO
- collect the KRLFS data, and clean (that is, check for and correct inconsistencies and other errors) and validate the data
- analyze the KRLFS to assess key labor force outcomes
- make recommendations for a KRI establishment survey.

A central component of the study was a series of workshops organized around the life cycle of the survey. RAND team members with expertise in survey data collection and analysis methods conducted survey-related workshops for KRSO staff and other government analysts over three separate trips to the KRI. The workshops were designed to be instructive and interactive.

Figure 5.1 shows the five steps of the survey process, each of which was the subject of a separate workshop. We highlight some key components of this capacity-building process below.

Sampling

Sampling is the selection of a subset of individuals or households (the "sample") from the larger population in order to estimate characteristics of the whole population. Sampling is significantly more cost-efficient than gathering information from every individual in the population, as a census would do. The science of sampling is well developed, and we adopted state-of-the-art techniques to carry out the KRLFS. The aim of the sampling strategy for the KRLFS was to carefully select the sample so that it is truly representative of the KRI population as a whole, including relevant regions or subgroups.

RAND staff conducted an intensive two-day workshop on sampling at KRSO in February 2012. The topics covered included ensuring that the sample is representative of the KRI population, deciding how large a sample is needed, and determining whether certain populations needed to be "oversampled" (sampled in larger numbers than would occur randomly to ensure that these populations are included in the sample).

Figure 5.1
The Survey Process and Structure of RAND Workshops for KRSO

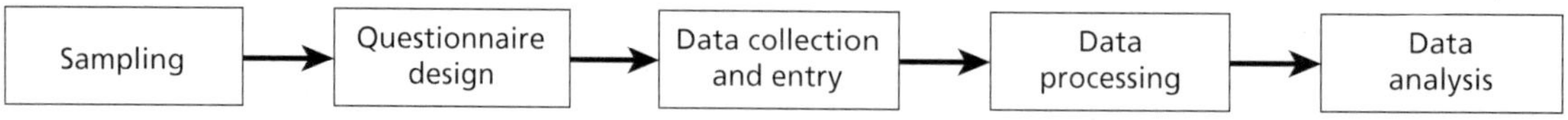

RAND *RR873-5.1*

Following the workshop, RAND worked in consultation with the KRSO to generate the sample. This process resulted in a sampling design that constitutes best international practice for labor force surveys, and through quarterly survey rounds will provide timely and reliable data to policymakers and the public. Further, since it is expected that the survey will be repeated every quarter, skills in sampling techniques will be reinforced over time.

Questionnaire Design

The questionnaire design workshop, conducted in February 2012, covered a range of issues that need to be considered when designing a survey, such as what questions should be asked and how they should be asked. The workshop discussed best practices and common mistakes in questionnaire designs and provided real-world examples.

Following the workshop, RAND and KRSO staff worked together to design the questionnaire for the KRLFS. The survey design was intended to meet three objectives:

- to provide useful and timely data to inform policymaking
- to provide information that is internationally comparable
- to achieve these objectives while keeping respondent burden (time required to complete the interview) reasonable.

The questionnaire was developed according to international best practices, including International Labour Organization guidelines for measuring labor force characteristics. This ensures both that the data are of high quality and that they can be used for international comparisons.

Data Collection, Cleaning, and Validation

An important step in developing a survey is to ensure that a process is in place to check for and correct errors. The data collection component of the study was critical to producing a high-quality data set for the KRLFS. RAND supported this process through workshops conducted in May 2012. A data collection workshop focused on best practices and challenges related to data collection, while a data cleaning and management workshop focused on the process of managing and using data, including ensuring confidentiality, checking for and correcting errors (data "cleaning"), and documenting results. Following the workshops, the RAND and KRSO teams communicated closely as the data collection and checking process progressed.

Data Analysis

In late July 2012, shortly after data collection and prior to analysis, RAND led two workshops for the KRSO focusing on labor market concepts and indicators, and statistical analysis of labor force data. The goal of the workshops was to enable the KRSO staff to conduct independent analysis of labor force surveys.

Coordination of Workshops with Survey Implementation

All workshops were closely integrated with the development and implementation of the KRLFS and were designed and timed to coincide with critical steps in the survey process. Workshops were also mutually reinforcing, often referring back to material covered in previous sessions.

The Kurdistan Region Labor Force Survey Provides Data on the Labor Market and Labor-Market Conditions

The KRLFS was designed and set up to be implemented on a recurring, quarterly basis. This will ultimately provide the government and public in the KRI with reliable, regularly updated information on the labor force and labor-market conditions to support policy decisionmaking. Below, we highlight some of the key findings from the first round of the survey (conducted in July 2012).

Labor Force Participation

The *labor force* is defined as the total number of individuals 15 years and older who are "economically active," meaning that they are currently either (1) working or (2) not working but available and actively searching for work. *Work* is defined, following international conventions, to include having a wage job or working on one's own, in a family business, or on a farm, whether directly for pay or not. It is international practice to classify as working or *employed* those who worked for at least one hour in the week preceding the interview date. The percentage of the working age population that is in the labor force is the *labor force participation rate* (see Figure 5.2).

The KRLFS data show that overall participation in the labor force is low in the KRI—just 38 percent of adults age 15 and older. Though this rate is essentially the same as in Jordan

Figure 5.2
Labor Force Status of the KRI Population and Definitions of Terms

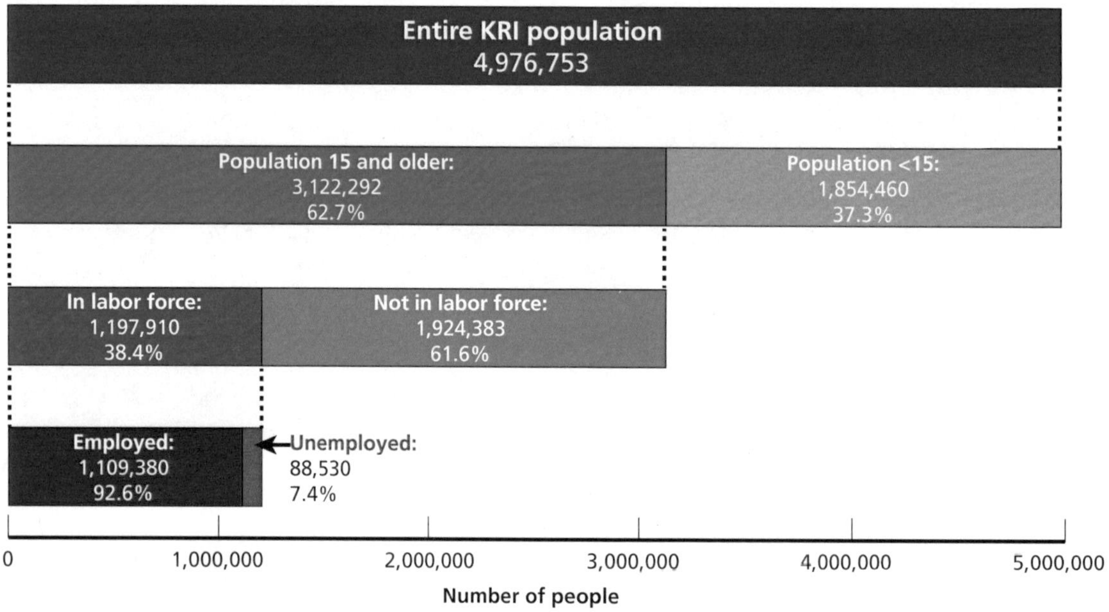

SOURCE: KRLFS.
NOTES: *In labor force* includes both the employed and the unemployed. The labor force participation rate is the number in the labor force divided by the population 15 and older. The unemployment rate is the number unemployed divided by the number in the labor force. The employed-to-population ratio is the number employed divided by the population 15 and older. The unemployment to population ratio is the number unemployed divided by the population 15 and older.
RAND *RR873-5.2*

(38 percent), it is significantly lower than in Turkey (approximately 50 percent) and Egypt (approximately 48 percent).

The low overall participation rate is driven in large part by very low participation of women (about 12 percent). Among men 15 years and older, about two-thirds, or nearly 66 percent, were in the labor force. However, among male youth (ages 15–24), only about 38 percent were in the labor force, largely because many were still studying. For female youth, the participation rate was only about 6 percent.

Employment Rate, Unemployment, and Underemployment

The labor force comprises two groups of individuals: those who are working (i.e., employed) and those who are not working but are willing and available to work and are also searching for work (the unemployed). In the KRI in the third quarter of 2012, 92.6 percent of the labor force was employed, whether full- or part-time (see Figure 5.2). This group makes up 35.5 percent of the total KRI population age 15 years and older.

Unemployment Rate by Age, Gender, and Education

The unemployment rate for a particular subset of the population equals the number of unemployed people in that group divided by the number in the labor force from that group. The unemployment rates for youth in particular are closely watched, because these indicate whether the economy is generating economic opportunities for those groups, thereby aiding both economic growth and social stability.

Within the KRI, youth unemployment (ages 15–24) is 17.6 percent, significantly higher than the 7.4 percent rate for the entire labor force (Figure 5.3). The phenomenon of high youth unemployment is well known in the Middle East. However, as with unemployment overall, youth unemployment in the KRI is among the lowest in the region. The comparable unem-

Figure 5.3
Unemployment Rate, by Age Group and Gender

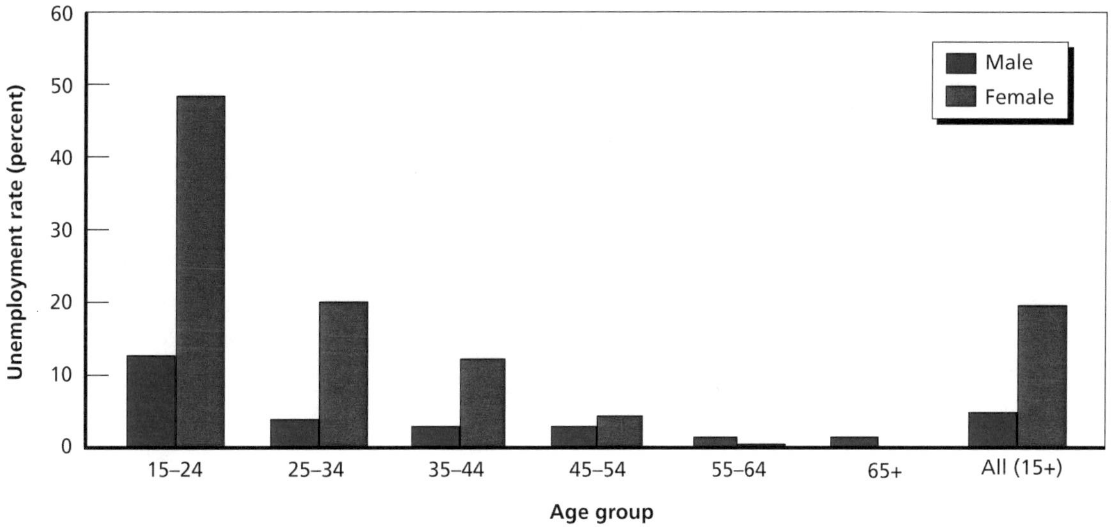

SOURCE: KRLFS.
RAND *RR873-5.3*

ployment rates for the 15–24 age group in the second quarter of 2012 were 16.1 percent in Turkey, 35.8 percent in Syria, and 28 percent in Jordan. The unemployment rate in Egypt for those aged 2024 was 41.4 percent in 2012 (this rate, however, is partially a reflection of the effects of the 2011 revolution on the economy).[1]

Further, gender differences in youth unemployment are noteworthy, as seen in Figure 5.3. In the KRI, the unemployment rate for female youth is much higher, at 48.9 percent, compared with 12.8 percent for young men. Despite the higher unemployment rate for young women, however, the actual number of unemployed young men is higher than the number of unemployed young women, because many fewer young women are in the labor force. The higher unemployment rates for women, particularly young women, suggest that females entering the workforce face difficulties in getting hired. Further, the low participation rate of young women (and women overall) noted earlier may also be evidence of such difficulties, if many young women do not enter or stay in the labor force because of difficulties in finding work.

For older age groups, unemployment is significantly lower for both men and women but is still generally much higher for women than men. For example, the unemployment rate for those aged 25 to 34 is 20.2 percent for females but 3.8 percent for males. The lowest unemployment rate is for those aged 55 to 64, for whom it is 1.5 percent overall and similar for both genders.

Finally, Table 5.1 considers patterns by rural or urban location and education level. Labor force participation and unemployment rates are both higher in urban areas, but modestly so. Participation is very high for those with a college degree (80 percent) and substantially lower for those with less education, especially secondary completers (41 percent).

Unemployment rates are also higher among those who are better educated. One factor behind this pattern is likely to be that those with more education tend to hold out for specific kinds of highly skilled jobs and have more family resources to support them while searching for work.

Table 5.1
Labor Force Participation and Unemployment, by Area and Education, Age 15+

	Labor Force Participation (%)	Unemployment (%)
Rural areas	35.3	6.0
Urban areas	39.0	7.7
Primary education	53.6	6.9
Secondary education	41.3	8.5
College degree	80.3	10.9

SOURCE: KRLFS.

[1] Data for the full age group of 15–24 year olds are unavailable for Egypt. Data for Turkey and Egypt are for the second quarter of 2012, while those for Syria are for 2011.

Other Characteristics of the KRI Labor Force and Economy

Results from the first KRLFS also highlighted other characteristics of the KRI labor force and economy, including the dominance of the public sector as a source of employment and the contrasting small role of the formal private sector; and the predominant role of service-sector employment, which accounts for three-quarters of all work, compared with less than 20 percent for industry. It is noteworthy that the vast majority—91 percent—of jobs defined as "formal" in the KRI are in the public sector; this includes the significant military sector.

Conclusions and Next Steps

Subsequent rounds of the KRLFS (which have been ongoing) will provide up-to-date information on how these and other important indicators are changing over time and in response to policies. At the same time, continued implementation of the survey will help to enhance KRSO's capabilities in data collection, analysis, and reporting, and prepare the basis for other survey collection efforts to meet specific needs for information.

Looking ahead, we recommend the following steps to build on the successful implementation of the KRLFS and other areas of progress made so far:

- Implement subsequent rounds of the KRLFS, adhering to a regular, quarterly schedule.
- Deepen the KRSO analytical capabilities, through future workshops and other means, to cover other topics that will enhance both analysis and reporting.
- Maintain and upgrade any capacity built through such means as workshops, training sessions, higher degree programs in foreign universities, and continuing learning.
- Consider investigating other topics of policy interest, including the determinants of wages and earnings in different sectors of the labor market and for different groups (for example, public- versus private-sector pay).
- Work with the KRSO to be able to flexibly identify and address other critical areas via appropriate data collection and analysis.
- Support the KRSO in leading the survey effort necessary to calculate the GRP and to develop the capacity for generating GRP and other key statistics from these surveys.

The KRG will need to collect new surveys as well as use existing surveys and other data sources in order to accurately calculate the GRP. RAND can continue to work with and build the capacity of the KRSO via workshops and communication on data collection, analysis, and reporting on this and other critical topics.

References

Berry, Sandra H., Nicholas Burger, Harun Dogo, Krishna B. Kumar, Alessandro Malchiodi, Jeffrey Martini, Tewodaj Mengistu, Howard J. Shatz, Alexandria C. Smith, Artur Usanov, and Joanne K. Yoong, *Designing a System for Policy-Relevant Data Collection for the Kurdistan Region-Iraq*, Santa Monica, Calif.: RAND Corporation, MG-1184-KRG, January 2012. As of October 8, 2014:
http://www.rand.org/pubs/monographs/MG1184-1.html

Cedefop, *Trends in VET Policy in Europe: 2010–2012*, Luxembourg: Publications Office of the European Union, 2012.

Eurobarometer, *Attitudes Toward Vocational Education and Training*, Special Report 369, European Commission, 2011. As of April 15, 2013:
http://ec.europa.eu/public_opinion/archives/ebs/ebs_369_en.pdf

Hansen, Michael L., Howard J. Shatz, Louay Constant, Alexandria C. Smith, Krishna B. Kumar, Heather Krull, Artur Usanov, Harun Dogo, and Jeffrey Martini, *Strategies for Private-Sector Development and Civil-Service Reform in the Kurdistan Region–Iraq*, Santa Monica, Calif.: RAND Corporation, MG-1117-KRG, 2011. As of October 8, 2014:
http://www.rand.org/pubs/monographs/MG1117-1.html

Johanson, Richard, *Sub-Sahara Africa (SSA): Regional Response to Bank TVET Policy in the 1990s*, AFTH4, The World Bank, January 2002.

Joint Commission International, *Joint Commission International Accreditation Standards for Hospitals*, 4th ed., July 2010.

KRSO—*See* Kurdistan Regional Statistics Office.

Kurdistan Regional Statistics Office, *Kurdistan Region Labor Force Survey, 2012*, Erbil, Kurdistan Region–Iraq, 2012.

Ministry of Higher Education and Scientific Research, *Higher Education Features 2010–11*, Tunis: Studies, Planning and Programming Office, 2012.

Murray, Alexander, "The State of Knowledge on the Role and Impact of Labour Market Information: A Survey of the International Evidence," CSLS Research Report 2010-05, June 2010. As of November 15, 2012:
http://scholar.googleusercontent.com/scholar?q=cache:s515_ocvPXUJ:scholar.google.com/+LMIS+%22Labor+Market+Information+System%22+&hl=en&as_sdt=0,5&as_ylo=2008

RAND Corporation, *RAND Survey of Business Establishments* (RAND Skills Survey), Santa Monica, Calif., 2012.

UNESCO, *Participation in Formal Technical and Vocational Education and Training Programmes Worldwide: An Initial Statistical Study*, 2006. As of April 15, 2013:
http://www.unevoc.unesco.org/fileadmin/user_upload/pubs/UNEVOC_UIS_Report.pdf

United Nations Industrial Development Organization (UNIDO), INDSTAT2–2012 Edition, Data CD-ROM, Vienna, 2012.

United Nations Statistics Division, "International Standard Industrial Classification of All Economic Activities, Rev.3: Detailed Structure and Explanatory Notes," website, undated. As of June 21, 2013:
http://unstats.un.org/unsd/cr/registry/regcst.asp?Cl=2

Vernez, G., S. Culbertson, and L. Constant, *Strategic Priorities for Improving Access to Quality Education in the Kurdistan Region—Iraq*, Santa Monica, Calif.: RAND Corporation, PR-1140-KRG, 2012.

Wahab, Moayad Abdullah, and Mazin Yousif Petros, *Health Facilities in Erbil Governorate*, 4th ed., Planning Department, Directorate of Health, Kurdistan Regional Government Ministry of Health, August 2011. As of December 31, 2013:
http://www.dohhawler.org/merg2012/kashkolenglish.pdf

Woods, James F., and Christoper J. O'Leary, "Conceptual Framework for an Optimal Labour Market Information System: Final Report," Upjohn Institute Technical Report No. 07-022, Kalamazoo, Mich.: W.E. Upjohn Institute for Employment Research, 2006. As of November 15, 2012:
http://research.upjohn.org/up_technicalreports/22/